Lincoln Christian College

W9-CBA-517

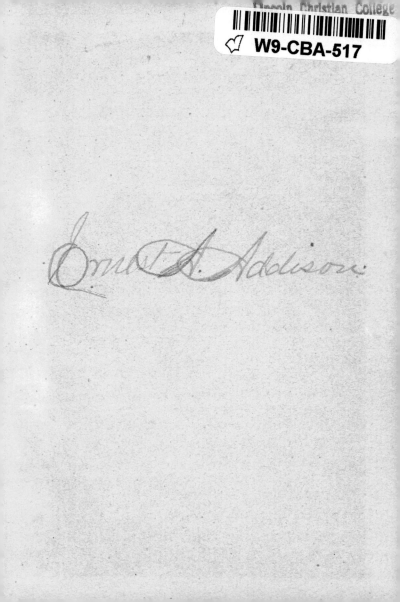

Ernest A. Addison

THE
NEW TESTAMENT
CHURCH

BY

HERBERT MONINGER
A. M., B. D.

Author of "Training for Service," "Who They
Are and What We Owe Them," "Graded
Supplemental Booklets," "Bible
Drills," "What's the
Answer?" etc.

FOR ADVANCED TEACHER-TRAINING
CLASSES, ADULT BIBLE
CLASSES, ETC.

═══════

ADDRESS ALL ORDERS TO
THE STANDARD PUBLISHING COMPANY
CINCINNATI, O.

COPYRIGHTED, 1908, BY THE STANDARD PUBLISHING COMPANY.

TABLE OF CONTENTS

PAGE.

PREFACE 3

INTRODUCTORY WORD.................................... 4

I. THE BOOKS OF THE BIBLE AND METHODS FOR STUDY-
   ING THEM...................................... 5

II. THE CHRIST OF THE NEW TESTAMENT CHURCH
    ACCORDING TO MATTHEW......................... 14

III. THE CHRIST OF THE NEW TESTAMENT CHURCH
     ACCORDING TO MARK............................ 21

IV. THE CHRIST OF THE NEW TESTAMENT CHURCH
    ACCORDING TO LUKE............................ 29

V. THE CHRIST OF THE NEW TESTAMENT CHURCH
   ACCORDING TO JOHN............................ 37

VI. THE HISTORY OF THE NEW TESTAMENT CHURCH.
    (A study of the Book of Acts)................. 43

VII. REVIEW 55

VIII. THE NEW TESTAMENT CHURCH AND THE NAME... 56

IX. THE NEW TESTAMENT CHURCH AND THE CREED.... 60

X. THE NEW TESTAMENT CHURCH AND CONVERSION.... 64

XI. THE NEW TESTAMENT CHURCH AND BAPTISM,...... 69

XII. THE NEW TESTAMENT CHURCH AND THE LORD'S
     SUPPER................... 77

XIII. THE NEW TESTAMENT CHURCH AND THE HOLY
      SPIRIT................................... 83

XIV. THE NEW TESTAMENT CHURCH AND ORGANIZA-
     TION 89

XV. THE NEW TESTAMENT CHURCH AND FINANCES.... 96

XVI. THE NEW TESTAMENT CHURCH AND MISSIONS.... 102

XVII. THE NEW TESTAMENT CHURCH AND JUDGMENT.. 106

XVIII. THE NEW TESTAMENT CHURCH AND CHRISTIAN
       UNION.. 114

XIX. RESTORATION OF THE NEW TESTAMENT CHURCH.. 122

XX. WINNING MEN TO THE NEW TESTAMENT CHURCH. 132

XXI. RAPID-FIRE DRILL QUESTIONS 137

XXII. ANSWERS TO RAPID-FIRE DRILL QUESTIONS..... 149

PREFACE

We have been more than surprised at the immediate reception given to our first standard teacher-training book, called " Training for Service." As many of those who have taken a part or all of this, or some other teacher-training course, will want to pursue the work further, we venture to place before the Bible-school world another book which is the first in a series of books on the *advanced* teacher-training work.

In this book we make a study of the New Testament church from various standpoints. It is a plea for the restoration of the New Testament church, in name, in ordinances and in life. Thinking that, perhaps, there will be some who will not care to use this book in union classes, we have prepared another one called "Studies in the Gospels and Acts." That book contains the first seven lessons that are found in this book, together with studies on the parables and miracles.

We have followed in this volume, as we did in "Training for Service," the plan of putting drill questions and answers in the back of the book for concert drill-work and Bible-knowledge contests. These questions are not given to save study, but to direct it and make it more definite.

A part of the material that is found in this book was originally published in a pamphlet called "Outline Studies in the New Testament Church." Claude Percy Leach rendered valuable assistance in the preparation of that pamphlet, and we hereby gratefully acknowledge his help.

As this book goes forth, it is with the hope that it may have a rich and helpful ministry, and that those who study its contents may be led to catch a larger vision of Christ and his church, and may through this vision be inspired to render a larger and richer service for the great Teacher of teachers.   H. M.

AN INTRODUCTORY WORD

As the first standard teacher-training book, called "Training for Servic," has been received with a most hearty welcome by fully one hundred thousand Bible students, we are encouraged to put out an advanced course that shall be a continuation of this training-work. THE ADVANCED STANDARD TEACHER-TRAINING COURSE is to cover two years and to be made up of one hundred lessons. This book contains the first twenty lessons of the first year's advanced course.

In this first year's work there are three books, which total the fifty required lessons:

THE NEW TESTAMENT CHURCH (this book)...... 20 lessons.
OLD TESTAMENT HISTORY, by C. S. Medbury.... 20 lessons.
A BIBLE-SCHOOL VISION, by P. H. Welshimer.... 10 lessons.

The second year's work has not as yet been completed, but it will be ready by the time any have completed the first year's course.

All persons who have taken, or are taking, the first standard teacher-training course should take up this *advanced* work. As soon as you have organized your class, enroll with your State or Provincial association. If you do not know the name of the general secretary of the Sunday-school work of your State or Province, write to the teacher-training department of the International Sunday-school Association, Room 806, Hartford Bldg., Chicago, Ill. An examination is given upon the completion of each book, and when the entire one hundred lessons are completed, an advanced standard teacher-training diploma will be granted. Both the examination questions and the diplomas are sent out from the general secretary of the Sunday-school work in your State.

THE NEW TESTAMENT CHURCH

LESSON I.

The Books of the Bible, and Methods for Studying Them

I. THE OLD TESTAMENT BOOKS

1. The Meaning of the Word.—The word "testament" means will or covenant. *Testamentum* is the Latin word.

2. The Purpose.—The old Testament is

(1) A book of history.

(2) It shows how God dealt with men in olden times.

(3) It shows how God chose a people through whom he might teach the worship of the one God, and through whom, in the fullness of time, he might send his Son to redeem the world.

But when the fulness of time came, God sent forth his Son, born of a woman, born under the law, that he might redeem them that were under the law, that we might receive the adoption of sons (Gal. 4 : 4, 5).

(4) It is the prophetic photograph of Christ.

(5) It is the schoolmaster that brings us to Christ.

So that the law is become our tutor *to bring us* unto Christ, that we might be justified by faith (Gal. 3 : 24).

5

3. The Divisions.—

(1) *Historical Books.* The first seventeen books are historical. They are generally subdivided into early and later history, or into the *Pentateuch* and books of *History.*

The three names given for the first five books of the Old Testament are *Law, Pentateuch, Early History.* They are called the *Law* because they contain the law as given at Mount Sinai. They are called the *Pentateuch,* as that is the Greek word meaning fivefold book. They are called *Early History* in contrast with the later history that begins with Joshua.

(2) *Devotional Books.* After the books of History, we have five books of Devotion, which have generally been called poetical books. These are Job, Psalms, Proverbs, Ecclesiastes and Song of Solomon.

(3) *Prophetical Books.* The last seventeen books of the Old Testament are prophetical. These books are subdivided into *Major Prophets* and *Minor Prophets.* There are five books of the former and twelve of the latter. These books of prophecy supplement the historical books.

II. THE NEW TESTAMENT BOOKS

The New Testament books cover the history of the first century following the birth of Christ. These books are divided into five sections.

1. The Gospels.—The four Gospels were written to prove that Jesus is the Christ, the Son of God, and our Saviour.

But these are written, that ye may believe that Jesus is the Christ, the Son of God; and that believing ye may have life in his name (John 20:31).

The Gospels were written by those whose names they bear. Matthew and John were apostles.

2. The Acts.—The Book of Acts tells of the foundation of the church and how we are to become Christians. This book was written by Luke, a close companion of Paul.

3. The Special and General Letters.—The Special and General Letters tell the people of all times how to live as Christians.

(1) *The Special Letters* are: Romans, 1 Corinthians, 2 Corinthians, Galatians, Ephesians, Philippians, Colossians, 1 Thessalonians, 2 Thessalonians, 1 Timothy, 2 Timothy, Titus, Philemon, Hebrews, These were written (except Hebrews) by the apostle Paul. The authorship of the Book of Hebrews is uncertain. It is placed among the Pauline letters because it is Pauline in teaching.

(2) *The General Letters* are: James, 1 Peter, 2 Peter, 1 John, 2 John, 3 John, Jude. These letters were written by those whose names they bear.

NOTE.—Second and Third John are classed under the "General" Letters, although they were written to individual Christians. Hebrews is also classed by some under the General Letters.

4. Prophecy.—(1) *Revelation.* The Book of Revelation tells of the future and the final triumph of the right. This book was written by the apostle John. It is called the *Apocalypse.*

III. METHODS OF BIBLE STUDY

The Bible is like the rich soil in the plains of Palestine, which yielded abundant harvests, notwithstanding the crude stick plows with which the Oriental farmer merely scratched the surface of the ground. The Scriptures will give up a wealth of helpfulness to the honest student, whatever may be his method. And yet one should not be satisfied with a spiritual yield which merely keeps one from starvation, when better methods might bring richer harvests for himself, and also to dispense to others for their growth (*The Sunday-school Teacher's Bible*).

Among the methods of Bible study, we call attention here to five, each of which, while it has its advantages, is not sufficient in itself for the making of a thorough Bible student. All of these methods should be more or less applied by each reader.

1. Study the Bible as a Whole.—Read a whole book of the Bible at a sitting. Many of the books of the Bible may be easily read in an hour or two. It is not so much the question as to how rapidly you read it if you read it thoroughly. Strange to say, this is one of the last things that many Christians are willing to do. They will read many books about the Bible, but to read the Bible itself they do not do. We would not think of treating any other book in this manner. We are living in a time when we feel it an obligation to be acquainted with the best authors. Shall we say that Shakespeare or Emerson, or any other great writer, is able to interest us in what he has written, when the Author of all life is unable to do so? Certainly we are not prepared to say that God, through holy men, can not write a book as capable of holding our attention and as fascinatingly interesting as any book that man has written unaided.

Dr. James M. Gray, of the Moody Bible Institute, tells this story, which is to the point here:

"I know a lady who once traveled a long distance on a railroad with her trunk unlocked, and when she met her husband at the terminus, and reported the circumstance, there was naturally some emotion in her speech. She had been unable to find the key anywhere, she said, and only discovered its loss at too late a moment to have another fitted before she started upon her journey. And the trunk, with all its treasures, had come that whole distance with only a strap around it. 'Why,' exclaimed her husband, 'do you not recall that when we come home from a journey I always fasten the key of the trunk to one of its handles? There's your key,' pointing to the end of the trunk."

The incident is recalled by the so frequent inquiry one hears for a "key" to the Bible. Its Author has provided one; and to the average person, at least in this enlightened country, it is always at hand. *Read the Book.*

2. Study the Bible by Books.—Take one book at a time, and read it over and over again with different points of view in mind. In order to really master a book, it should be read several times rather than laying it aside and passing on to a second book. A visitor to our Capital City, in looking down from the top of Washington monument on a foggy morning, could scarcely believe there was a city below. Later, however, when the sun rises and the fog

begins to disappear, there appears at first the tops
of some of the highest buildings and the steeples
of the churches; then the outline of the streets, then
the factories and stores, and thousands of trees and
the beautiful parks, stand out in beauty. It is much
the same way in making an inductive study of
the Bible. The first view, while helpful, is not com-
pletely satisfactory. By looking and re-looking, however, new thoughts appear, and the whole book presents a new and richer meaning.

This method is briefly illustrated in the following example:

"The Book of Ruth has been chosen for study.
Let it be read in its entirety, first for the simple
and beautiful story which it tells. Then, a more
careful study of its features will disclose that it is
a most engaging idyllic prose poem; parts of it ris-
ing to the heights of pure Hebrew poetry, with its
balancing of line against line in complete parallel-
ism. Romance follows tragedy. The struggle to
'keep the wolf from the door' in days of famine;
love, marriage, death, widowhood, follow in rapid
succession. Embers of a latent patriotism and religious fealty burn bright again; motherly solicitude
and filial piety shine forth as if to vie with each
in brilliant loyalty. A maidenlike coyness and a
maternal intrigue; a love at first sight and a happy,
fruitful marriage—all these go into the making of
this divinely inspired pastoral.

"Read again and carefully study the historical
setting of the book. Find its niche in the life of
God's chosen people. It was 'in the days when the

judges ruled.' See Moab, destined to play no unimportant part in later history; and the famine, which, not uncommon, again and again played a providential role in the shaping of human destinies; the intermarriage with heathen people, not so strictly under the ban as at a later period; Oriental customs and Hebrew laws of the harvest; laws of consanguinity and inheritance; the levirate marriage; the custom of the 'loosed shoe;' Ruth an ancestress of David and so of the Messiah."

3. Study the Bible Biographically.—Even the casual reader of the Bible will find that most of the truths it contains are impersonated in some life. The events of the Old Testament, as well as those of the New, may be grouped around certain personalities. In our first Standard teacher-training book, entitled "Training for Service," we have endeavored, in Chapters VI. and VII., to group all of the Old Testament history around sixteen major and forty-eight minor characters. The Gospels are hinged around the Master's life. The events of the Book of Acts may be grouped around three men, Peter, Philip and Paul. This method of study not only makes the Bible more interesting, but makes its facts and truths more easily remembered.

4. Study the Bible According to Institutions of Worship and Service.—There have been five institutions of worship since the beginning of history. These are altar, tabernacle, temple, synagogue and church. To follow the origin, the plan, purpose and practice of each of these institutions will not only show how the Lord has been and is worshiped, but will reveal how to some extent each institution of worship is a fulfillment of the preceding ones. The studies that are to follow in this book are largely those that have to do with the church.

This plan of studying the Bible through institutions of worship includes to some extent another plan of Bible study that may be called the *Topical Method*. For example, one may wish to know the teachings of the Bible on the subject of the "Atonement." This subject naturally includes the discussion of the institutions of worship and service. Another subject would be that universal question, "How may one be saved?"

5. Study the Bible Devotionally.—All proper methods of Bible study help the devotional life. As some studies, however, have for them a more intellectual purpose, we should from time to time study the Bible with the spiritual pre-eminently in mind. In this study one meditates upon certain passages, not only until he gets hold of them, but until they get hold of him. He studies them and yields himself to them until he "knows them by heart." In such a method of studying the Word one hears the still small voice, and the soul hunger is satisfied by spiritual manna. After one has followed this method of study awhile, he can understand the exclamation of the Psalmist:

> "Oh how I love thy law !
> It is my meditation all the day."

SOME REFERENCE BOOKS

First Principles, by M. M. Davis, Chapter III.; *How to Master the English Bible*, by James M. Gray;

A Guide to Bible Study, by J. W. McGarvey; *Helpful Bible Readings*, by A. B. Moore; *Bible Study Popularized*, by Frank T. Lee.

TOPICS FOR CLASS DISCUSSION

1. The meaning of the word "testament."

2. The relation of the Old and New Testaments.

3. The three names of the first five books of the Old Testament.

4. The joint purpose of the four Gospels.

5. The purpose of the Book of Acts.

6. The purpose of the Special and General Letters.

7. The purpose of the Book of Revelation.

8. If a person did not believe in Christ, to which books of the Bible would you refer him? Why?

9. If a person already believed in the divinity of Christ, to which book would you refer him that he might know how to become a Christian? Why?

10. Plans that will aid in mastering the English Bible.

11. Some guides to Bible study.

12. The value of a concordance in Bible study. (The person who is assigned this topic should bring with him a good concordance, such as Young's, Walker's or Cruden's.)

13. The value of a Bible Dictionary in Bible study. (The person to whom this subject is assigned should show the class some good Bible dictionary.)

14. The value of a good reference Bible. (The person discussing this subject should have in his hand a good reference Bible and tell how to use the references.)

RAPID-FIRE DRILL

Use Questions 1-12 inclusive, in the back of this book.

BLACKBOARD OUTLINE

I. O. T. BOOKS.	II. N. T. BOOKS.	III. METHODS OF BIBLE STUDY.
1. Mea. of Wd.	1. The Gospels.	
2. Purpose.	2. Acts.	1. As a whole.
3. Divisions.	3. Spec. and Gen. Letters.	2. By books.
(1) Historical.	4. Prophecy.	3. Biographically.
(2) Devotional.		4. By institutions.
(3) Prophetic.		5. Devotional.

LESSON II.

The Christ of the New Testament Church According to Matthew

I. THE AUTHOR

The Gospel which bears the name of Matthew was written by the apostle.

1. His Name.—Matthew is the same as Levi (Luke 5: 27-29), the son of Alpheus. He is not to be confused with Matthias, who was chosen to take the place of Judas.

2. His Occupation.—Matthew was a tax-gatherer at Capernaum. His special duty was likely to collect tolls from the fishers on the Lake of Galilee, and perhaps from merchants traveling southward from Damascus. His duties as a tax-gatherer would bring him into disrepute with his countrymen, who disliked all agents of the foreign despotism under which they groaned.

3. His Character.—Matthew, because of his position, was likely a man of means. He was a modest man and kept himself well in the background. Being a man of means, it meant a great deal for him to forsake all to follow Jesus.

4. His Call.—Matthew's call to be an apostle is related by Matthew, Mark and Luke in practically the same words (Matt. 9: 9; Mark 2: 14; Luke 5: 27). One day Jesus was coming up from the Lake of Galilee and passed near the custom-house where Matthew was seated in Oriental fashion, and he said unto him, "Follow me." Matthew arose and followed Christ.

5. His Position Among the Twelve.—Matthew does not shine out in his work as do Peter, James and John. He, however, was a most faithful apostle, and, according to tradition, died the death of a martyr.

6. The Date of His Gospel.—Because of the use of such expressions as "holy city," "holy place," "the city of the great king" (4: 5; 5: 35; 24: 15; 27: 53), and from the nature of the language used by our Saviour in his prediction of the city's coming doom, Dr. J. A. McClymont holds that Matthew's Gospel was written before 66 A. D., when the war which was to issue in the destruction of the Jewish capital was on the eve of breaking out. McGarvey holds that it was not written before 60 A. D., and was probably written about 67 A. D.

II. CHARACTERISTICS OF THE GOSPEL

1. Language of the Gospel.—According to Origen, Eusebius, Jerome and many others, Matthew's Gospel was written in Hebrew (*i. e.*, Aramaic, the vernacular language of Palestine). It was afterwards translated into Greek. Irenæus says, "Matthew among the Hebrews brought out a writing of the Gospel in their own tongue." Eusebius in the beginning of the fourth century says that Matthew wrote it when he was about to leave the Jews and preach also to other nations in order to "fill up the void about to be made in his absence." If it be true that Matthew wrote his Gospel in Aramaic, it very soon also appeared in Greek. Whether Matthew wrote the Gospel over again in Greek, or whether some other person translated it, is a question we can not answer.

2. Written for the Jews.—Matthew introduces Jesus as the Messiah, or the Christ. His main purpose was to set forth the Messiahship of Jesus rather than his divinity. The first verse of the book opens with the words, "The book of the generation of Jesus Christ, the son of David, the son of Abraham." By this Matthew designates Christ as the promised seed of David, who was to sit on David's throne and reign forever, and he also keeps in mind the promise to Abraham of a seed in whom all the nations of the world were to be blessed. "No one can read Matthew's Gospel without perceiving that he was no Hellenist, but a Hebrew of the Hebrews, deeply learned in the history and prophecies of his race, and eagerly looking forward to their realization.

When the plan and teaching of Jesus were unfolded to his mind stored with national memories, he instantly recognized the truth and beauty and completeness of that ideal, and gave himself up heart and soul to the cause of the son of David. For that cause and for the kingdom of God he resigned all his hopes of advancement in Herod's kingdom, his lucrative calling, and the friends he had made." —*Cambridge Bible.* This gives one explanation of Matthew's intense desire to present Jesus as the Messiah of the Jews.

The following points gathered by Dr. A. Carr indicate that Matthew's Gospel had special reference to the Jews, and that he represented Jesus as the Messianic hope realized.

(1) The appeals to history as fulfilled in Christ.

(2) The rare explanation of Jewish words and customs.

(3) The strong and special denunciation of the Jews and of their rulers.

(4) The special reference to the Law in the Sermon on the Mount.

(5) The genealogy traced from Abraham and David.

(6) The mission of the Seventy omitted.

(7) The absence of Latin words, with very few exceptions.

(8) The prominence given to the Jewish thought of a kingdom or heaven: (*a*) in the general scope of the Gospel; (*b*) in the parables; (*c*) in the account of the Passion.

3. Filled with Old Testament Quotations.—In the

course of Matthew's Gospel there are no less than sixty quotations from the Old Testament prophecy as fulfilled in Jesus. Since Matthew's aim is to show that Jesus is the fulfillment of Messianic hopes, we would naturally expect just this. The designation "son of David" occurs seven times as applied to Jesus.

4. Matthew Represents Christ as the Teacher of Teachers.—The best book on pedagogy that has been written is the Gospel of Matthew. Matthew seeks the "point of contact" with the Jews by beginning his Gospel in writing the genealogy of Christ from Abraham to his birth in Bethlehem. He shows how Christ complimented his hearers before he corrected them (Matt. 5: 17). In the Sermon on the Mount, given in more or less detail by Matthew, he represents Jesus as speaking as "never a man spake." When we want abstract teaching, we turn to Matt. 5: 3-12. When we want good illustrations, we turn to Matt. 5: 13-16. When we want to know how to use parables in teaching, we read Matt. 13: 1-53. There is scarcely a principle in teaching but what is used in some striking way in the Gospel of Matthew.

In the six principles of teaching given below, see how they are illustrated by the Scripture cited.

(1) *Put the new in an old setting.* Matt. 1: 1-23.

(2) *Use words that are understood by the teacher and the scholar in the same sense.* Matt. 5: 12, 40, 41.

(3) *Adapt the teaching to the needs of the scholars.* Matt. 13: 3-9, 18-30.

(4) *Secure co-operation.* Matt. 16: 13-19.

(5) *The development of the subject must con-*

stantly present new points of interest. See Sermon on the Mount (Matt. 5, 6, 7).

(6) *Ideas must be repeated to be retained.* Matt. 16: 21; 17: 23; 20: 17-19; 26: 2.

5. Matthew Emphasizes the Words of Jesus.—In comparing Matthew and Mark, we often see that Mark emphasizes the *works* of Jesus, while Matthew pays especial attention to his *words.* This is shown by the fact that Mark lays emphasis upon the miracles and Matthew upon the parables. The fact that Matthew lays emphasis upon the words of Jesus is also seen by his faithful account of the Sermon on the Mount and from the fact that considerably more than half his book is taken up with Christ's formal speeches, aside from many remarks made in conversation with friends and foes.

6. Matthew Emphasizes the Judgment.—There is an element of "sternness and severity" to Matthew's Gospel that does not appear elsewhere in the recorded teachings of Christ. Matthew alone records the parables of the judgment; *i. e.,* the tares, the dragnet, the ten virgins, the talents and the rejection of the goats. Matthew also records the denunciation of the scribes and Pharisees (23: 13-36). For the material given only by Matthew, see the Harmony of Christ's life found elsewhere in this book.

7. Matthew's Gospel Naturally Divides Itself.— In 4: 17 he says, "From that time began Jesus to preach;" and in 16: 21, "From that time began Jesus to show unto his disciples, that he must go unto Jerusalem, and suffer many things from the elders and chief priests and scribes, and be killed, and the third day be raised up." Thus we see that Matthew has himself marked the natural divisions of the book. The threefold division, then, is:

(1) *Genealogy of Christ.* Matt. 1: 1-4: 16.

(2) *Christ's Active Ministry.* Matt. 4: 17-16: 20.

(3) *The Closing Events of Christ's Life.* Matt. 16: 21-28: 20.

While the last division occupies scarcely more than six months of the three years and more of his ministry, yet the events of this period take nearly one-half of the book, showing the importance attached by Matthew to the scenes connected with the final suffering, the death, and the resurrection of the Christ. It is to be noticed that the contrast between 4: 17 and 16: 21 is most significant. The former is preceded by the baptism of Christ when from heaven a voice said, "This is my beloved Son, in whom I am well pleased" (Matt. 3: 17), and the latter is immediately followed by the transfiguration when the heavenly voice said, "This is my beloved Son, in whom I am well pleased; hear ye him" (Matt. 17: 5).

TOPICS FOR HOME STUDY AND CLASS DISCUSSION

1. How many times and under what circumstances is the apostle Matthew mentioned?

2. Discuss the position of tax-gatherer and what the community thought of one in such a business.

3. Give an outline of the Gospel according to Matthew.

4. Why does Matthew give such a long genealogy in the first chapter?

5. Why does Matthew give such a long account of the Sermon on the Mount?

6. What parables does Matthew give that are not given by any other Gospel writer?

7. Name five characteristics of Matthew's Gospel.

RAPID-FIRE DRILL

See Questions 13-30, inclusive, in the back of this book.

BLACKBOARD OUTLINE

I. THE AUTHOR.	II. CHARACTERISTIC OF GOSPEL.
1. His Na.	1. Lang. of Gos.
2. His Oc.	2. Writ. for Jews.
3. His Char.	3. Fi. with O. T. Quo.
4. His Call.	4. Rep. Chr. as Te. of Te.
5. Pos. Am. Twe.	5. Emph. Words of Jesus.
6. Date of Gos.	6. Emph. Judgment.
	7. Gos. Nat. Div. Its.

LESSON III.

The Christ of the New Testament Church According to Mark

I. THE AUTHOR

The second Gospel was written by John Mark, who was a companion of both the apostle Paul and the apostle Peter.

1. His Name.—There were three Johns in the New Testament that were especially prominent, John the Baptist, John the apostle and John Mark, the writer of the second Gospel. The last John men-

tioned is the one under consideration now. His
Jewish name was John and his Gentile name Mark,
or Marcus (Col. 4: 10; Philem. 24; 1 Pet. 5: 13). Marcus is supposed to be the Latin *"marcus,"* meaning
a hammer. As we study his Gospel, we must feel
that this is indeed a most appropriate name for him.
He was a strong hammer, able to crush the flint
rock; and this is indicative of the spiritual power
that the evangelist was able to wield. While Mark
is a Gentile name, he nevertheless was a Jew.
Throughout his entire Gospel he betrays his nationality and breathes the spirit of an Israelite, and
who, though too big to be bound within Jewish nar-
rowness and bigotry, was still "an Israelite indeed."

2. His Home Life.—Mark was not an apostle, but
was the son of a certain Mary in Jerusalem, whose
house was a place of resort for the disciples (Acts
12: 12). This Mary was an aunt of Barnabas, since
Mark was his cousin (Col. 4: 20). Mark grew up
in Jerusalem, where his mother was prominent
among the disciples. He probably was acquainted
with the apostles and may even have seen Jesus.

3. His Relation to Peter.—Peter calls John Mark
his son in the gospel (1 Pet. 5: 13). It can not be
a mere term of endearment, but perhaps means that
Mark was one of Peter's converts. The fact that
Peter, when he was miraculously released from
prison, went to the house of Mark's mother, may indicate that he was intimate with the family (Acts
12: 12). In early tradition Mark is represented as
the "interpreter of Peter," which may mean that he
accompanied him in the later years of the apostle's

life and acted as his spokesman when addressing Gentile audiences, or it may mean that Mark merely wrote down the things that Peter preached. As a confirmation of the fact that many of the things that Mark relates in his Gospel were those which Peter was in the habit of giving in his discourses, we note that he tells plainly many things that Peter did or said which were not a credit to him, and omits nearly all that was.

(1) It was Peter who followed after our Lord in the morning after the miracles at Capernaum (Mark 1: 36).

(2) It was he who drew attention to the rapid withering of the fig-tree (Mark 11: 21).

(3) It was he who, with three other of the apostles, asked our Lord, as he sat on the Mount of Olives, respecting the destruction of Jerusalem (Mark 13: 3).

(4) It was to him specially amongst the apostles to whom the angel directed that the announcement of the resurrection should be made (Mark 16: 7).

This is the way, likely, that Peter would have done. Mark often especially mentions Peter when the other evangelists omitted him.

As an illustration of Peter's modesty, showing that he was anxious to pass over what might especially redound to his honor, we find the omission of

(1) His name as the prompter of the question respecting "meats not defiling a man" (comp. Mark 7: 17 with Matt. 15:15).

(2) His walking on the sea (comp. Mark 6: 50, 51 with Matt. 14: 28-31).

(3) The miracle of the coin in the fish's mouth (comp. Mark 9: 33 with Matt. 17: 24-27).

(4) His designation as the rock, on which the church should be built (comp. Mark 8: 29, 30 with Matt. 16: 17-19).

(5) His being sent with another apostle to make ready the Passover (comp. Mark 14: 13 with Luke 22: 8).

(6) The fact that it was for *him* especially that our Lord prayed that his faith might not "utterly fail" (Luke 22: 31, 32).—*Maclear.*

4. His Relation to Paul.—Mark accompanied Barnabas and Paul from Jerusalem to Antioch in Syria (Acts 12: 25), and afterwards, when these two men started on their first missionary journey, Mark goes with them (Acts 13: 5). For some unstated reason, however, Mark leaves Paul and Barnabas at Perga and returns to Jerusalem. His motive may have been the fear for his mother's safety in Jerusalem, where all Christians were in danger of frequent persecution, or he may have feared the hardship of the inland trip into Asia Minor, or he may have taken ill. Whatever the reason for Mark's conduct, Paul disapproved of it so much that he refused to take him with them when a second missionary journey was proposed (Acts 15: 38). As a result of this contention, Barnabas and Mark sailed to Cyprus and resumed evangelistic work, and Paul takes Silas with him as he enters upon his second missionary tour. For about a decade Mark disappears from history. We next find him in Rome with Paul (Col. 4: 10), with whom he has again found

favor. During Paul's second imprisonment in Rome
he requests Timothy to bring Mark, saying that he
was useful to him for ministering (2 Tim. 4: 2).

5. The Date of the Gospel.—We may conclude
that it was written between 64 A. D. and 68 A. D.—
the latter being the year of Nero's death, in whose
reign Peter and Paul are believed to have suffered
martyrdom.—*McClymont.*

II. CHARACTERISTICS OF THE GOSPEL

1. The Shortest Gospel.—Mark occupies the least
space of any of the Gospel writers in giving his
picture of the Christ. His descriptions are brief,
straightforward and vivid.

2. Gentile Gospel.—While Matthew's Gospel is
saturated with quotations from the Old Testament
Scriptures, showing how Christ is a fulfillment of
them, Mark scarcely ever quotes prophecy. This
would lead us to the opinion that the Gospel was
not written especially for the Jews. The fact also
that Mark adds translations and explanations of
words that would be intelligible to the Jews would
also tell us that this is a Gentile Gospel. Examples
of such translations and explanations are found in
such expressions as "Boanerges—Sons of Thunder"·
(3: 17); "Bartimæus—the son of Timæus" (10: 46);
"Abba, Father" (14: 36); "Talitha cumi; which is,
being interpreted, Damsel, I say unto thee, Arise"
(5: 41). Customs are also frequently explained in
a manner that would not be necessary if the Gospel
had been written for the Jews (see 7: 3; 2: 18; 12:
18; 14: 12; 15: 6, 42).

As Mark's Gospel depicts Christ in all of his ener-
getic and victorious strength, we may say it is a
Gospel well fitted to impress the Roman mind. The
tradition that Mark wrote in Rome, that his Gospel
was for the Romans, is somewhat confirmed from
frequent use of Latin words, such as "denarius" (12:
15); "Prætorium" (15: 16); "centurion" (15: 39).

3. Mark's Descriptions are Most Vivid.—He describes the emotions, looks, gestures and actions of
Christ and of others (see 3: 5, 34; 7: 33; 8: 33; 9:
36; 10: 32). In the description of the feeding of the
five thousand, Mark alone tells us that they sat down
in ranks by hundreds and fifties upon the *green
grass.* In further evidence, note the "photographic
character" of Mark's account of the transfiguration
and of the storm on the Lake of Galilee. In still further keeping with this idea, we note that Mark has
carefully recorded the minute particulars which are
unnoticed by the other Gospel writers:

The person (1: 29; 2: 36; 3: 6; 3: 22; 11: 11, 21;
13: 3; 14: 65; 15: 21; 16: 7).

Number (5: 13; 6: 7, 40; 14: 30).

Time (4: 35; 6: 2; 11: 11, 19; 15: 25; 16: 2).

Place (4: 1; 5: 20; 13: 3; 14: 68; 15: 39; 16: 5).

4. Mark Emphasizes Christ as a Worker.—While
Matthew emphasizes him as a teacher, Mark says
that he came to *do* something as well as *say* something. This accounts for the fact that Matthew en-
larges upon the *words* of Christ, while Mark en-
larges upon his *works;* Matthew lays emphasis upon
his *parables* and Mark upon his *miracles.*

5. Christ is the Master Man of the Living

Present.—Matthew lays much emphasis upon the past in that he gives a full genealogy of Christ, quotes prophecy, etc. Mark sets Jesus before us as he worked and taught in the *living present*, a wonderful worker of miracles and a possessor of more than mortal authority. Mark's Gospel has a larger portion of common matter than any of the others. Fully 93 per cent. of the whole contents of Mark's Gospel is found in one or more of the other Gospels. "No one who is familiar with Matthew can read Mark without noticing a striking similarity between them in the facts that they relate, and sometimes in the words that they employ; but, on close comparison of the two, it will be seen that in almost, if not quite, all these instances, Mark has some additional items which distinguish his account from Matthew's. The student should constantly keep his eye open for these, for they not only show the difference between the two writers, making each stand out before the mind by himself, but they are necessary to a full knowledge of the incidents with which they are connected. The same may be said in reference to events mentioned by three, or by all, of the Gospel writers. Study all, and combine the particulars given by all."
—*McClymont.*

6. Mark's Purpose is to Prove the Divinity rather than the Messiahship of Jesus.—This main purpose is clearly put forth in his introductory words: *"The beginning of the Gospel of Jesus Christ, the Son of God."* In this Mark differs from Matthew, as it was Matthew's main purpose to prove that Christ is the Messiah of the Old Testament.

In carrying out that plan, Matthew devoted much space to prophecy and to the discourses of the Master. On the other hand, Mark, in carrying out his plan, devotes much space to the miracles, for in these, rather than through prophecy, he could prove his divinity. Mark begins his account of the life of Christ with the preaching of John the Baptist, while Matthew begins with the genealogy and birth of Christ. The reason for this is found in the distinction just given above.

TOPICS FOR HOME STUDY AND CLASS DISCUSSION

1. Mark's early life.

2. His Jewish name and his Roman name.

3. Name and designate three Johns in the New Testament.

4. What was Mark's relation to Barnabas?

5. What was Mark's relation to the apostle Peter?

6. What was Mark's relation to the apostle Paul?

7. Why is Mark's Gospel sometimes called the Petrine Gospel?

8. Name some things in Mark's Gospel that are peculiar to this Gospel.

9. Why does Mark explain Hebrew words or phrases?

10. What is Mark's purpose in writing his Gospel as compared with Matthew?

11. Name two characteristics of Mark's Gospel.

12. Give an outline of Mark's Gospel.

RAPID-FIRE QUESTIONS

See Questions 31-50, inclusive, in the back of this book.

BLACKBOARD OUTLINE

I. THE AUTHOR.	II. CHARACTERISTICS OF GOSPEL.
1. His Name.	1. Shortest Gos.
2. Ho. Life.	2. Gen. Gos.
3. Rela. to Pet.	3. Des. Mo. Viv.
4. Rela. to Paul.	4. Emp. Chr. as a Wo.
5. Date of Gos.	5. Ch. Mas. Man of Liv. Pre.
	6. Pro. Div. ra. th. Mes. of Jesus.

LESSON IV.

The Christ of the New Testament Church According to Luke

I. THE AUTHOR

The author of the third Gospel is Luke, a faithful companion of Paul.

1. His Name.—There are but three places in the Scripture where Luke's name is mentioned. In Col. 4: 14, Paul says, "Luke, the beloved physician, and Demas salute you." In 2 Tim. 4: 11, the same writer says, "Only Luke is with me;" and in Philemon 24 he is mentioned as one of Paul's "fellow-workers." While Luke is mentioned by name only in these three instances, yet we may learn much of him from the Book of Acts, in which he intimates his presence with Paul at times by the use of "we" or "us" in the narrative (Acts 16: 10-17; 20: 5-21: 18; 27: 1-28: 16).

2. His Early Life.—Early tradition says that Luke was a native of Antioch in Syria. Whether or not this is true, his interest in and his familiarity with the church at Antioch is evident. Note Acts 6: 5; 11: 19-27; 13: 1-3; 14: 26-28; 15: 1, 2, 30-40; 18: 22, 23. Ramsay, in his book called "St. Paul the Traveler," holds that Luke was a Philippian. Eusebius says: "Luke, who was born at Antioch, and by profession a physician, being for the most part connected with Paul, and familiarly acquainted with the rest of the apostles, has left us two inspired books. One of these is his Gospel, in which he testifies that he has recorded 'as those who were from the beginning eye-witnesses and ministers of the Word delivered unto him,' whom also, he says, he has in all things followed. . . . It is also said that Paul usually referred to his Gospel, whenever in his Epistles he spoke of some particular Gospel of his own, saying, 'according to my Gospel.'" Origen, quoted by Eusebius, writes: "And the third, according to Luke, the Gospel commended by Paul, which was written for the converts from the Gentiles." Irenæus refers frequently to Luke by name; as, "Luke, also the companion of Paul, recorded in a book the gospel preached by him."

3. His Profession.—Luke was a physician, and is called by Paul, "the beloved physician" (Col. 4: 14). Some have suggested that Luke traveled with Paul because the latter had need of medical attendance. Some traits of Luke's profession may be discovered in the frequency with which he refers to the work of Christ and that of his apostles as the ministry of healing (4: 18, 23; 9: 1, 2, 6; 10: 9); as well as the occasional use of expressions which a physician would likely employ (4: 38; 5: 12; 6: 19; 22: 44).

4. His Nationality.—Luke likely was not a Jew. From the distinction drawn between him and those "of the circumcision" (Col. 4: 11-14), "it may be inferred that he was of Gentile extraction, and this inference is confirmed by his Greek name and the character of his style, which—except when he is drawing from older documents or reporting speeches conveyed to him by others—is more classical than that of the other Gospels, alike as regards the structure of the sentences and the choice of words, as well as in his use of an opening dedication, a feature quite foreign to the Hebrew style."—*McClymont.* As Luke was not a Jew, he was the only Gentile to write any part of the New Testament. Of the Gospel writers, Matthew and John were apostles; Mark and Luke were not.

5. His Relation to Paul.—By reading the following passages, it will appear that Luke joined Paul on his second missionary journey at Troas, in Asia Minor, and went with him over to Philippi in Macedonia (Acts 16: 10-17; 20: 5-21: 18; 27: 1-28: 16). Again, on Paul's third journey, Luke rejoined the apostle at Philippi and went with him to Jerusalem. He likely remained in Palestine during the two years in which Paul was in prison at Cæsarea, and he sailed with the apostle from Cæsarea to Rome. When Paul is writing his last letter while in prison in Rome, after he has written those well-known words of having fought the good fight and having finished the course and having kept the faith, he tells about different ones who had left him, and says, "Luke only is with me" (2 Tim. 4: 11). Sometimes the third Gospel is called Paul's Gospel because it was written by one who was a very close companion of Paul, and no doubt writes in many ways as Paul would have written.

6. The Date of Luke's Gospel.—From Acts 1: 1 it is clear that it was written before the Book of Acts, which (see Acts 28: 30, 31) must have been completed before the end of the second year of Paul's imprisonment; that is, about A. D. 63.—*Thompson.*

II. CHARACTERISTICS OF THE GOSPEL

1. The Gospel of Sympathy.—(1) It is in this Gospel that we find a record of the visit of Christ to the house of Zaccheus, the publican (9: 1).

(2) It is here that we have his gracious reception of the woman who was a sinner (7: 37).

(3) It is here that we see his promise of paradise to the penitent thief (23: 43).

(4) Luke shows that Christ embraced within the range of his sympathy (*a*) the Gentile (4: 25-27; 23: 28, 29) and the (*b*) poor (2: 7, 8, 24; 6: 20; 9: 58; 14: 21).

(5) Christ cared for those whom the society of that time neglected or hated.

(*a*) For women (10: 38-42).

(*b*) For children (18: 17).

(*c*) For the despised (16: 19-22).

(*d*) For the social outcast (15: 1).

The breadth of Christ's sympathy is as wide as human need. The more urgent the need the greater is his outflow of sympathetic help. His ministry extends to the whole man, body, mind and soul.

> "The great Physician now is near,
>   The sympathizing Jesus.
> He speaks the drooping heart to cheer,
>   Oh! hear the voice of Jesus.
> Your many sins are all forgiv'n,
>   Oh! hear the voice of Jesus.
> Go on your way in peace to heaven
>   And wear a crown with Jesus."

2. Samaritan Gospel.—Luke tells how Christ shamed the "thankless Jews" by the example of the "thankful Samaritan" (17: 16). Through the parable of the good Samaritan recorded only by Luke, he shows how the good Samaritan surpasses the proud priest and Levite in his compassion upon one who had fallen among thieves. The priest and the Levite passed by on the other side, but the good Samaritan, moved with compassion, did something for the half-killed man. His compassion was more than a mere sentiment. It was that which led him to a merciful deed. Through this Samaritan parable all Christians are taught that the one who needs help is our neighbor.

3. Luke Emphasizes the Perean Ministry.—In Luke 9: 51-10: 14, we have a record of many of the activities of Christ preserved only by this writer. Some of the most precious parts of this Gospel are found here. A few of them are:

(1) Parable of the Great Supper (14: 15-24).

(2) Parable of the Lost Sheep (15: 3-7).

(3) Parable of the Lost Piece of Silver (15: 8-10).

(4) Parable of the Prodigal Son (15: 11-32).

(5) Parable of the Unjust Steward (16: 1-18).

(6) Parable of the Rich Man and Lazarus (16: 19-31).

(7) Parable of the Healing of the Ten Lepers (17: 12-19).

(8) The Pharisee and the Publican (18: 1-14).

Most of these events are included in Christ's Perean ministry, which occupies the larger part of the last three months of his life.

4. Luke Reveals the Sacredness of Infancy.—He alone tells of the birth and infancy of the Baptist; the Annunciation; the meeting of Mary and Elizabeth; the songs of the herald Angels; the Circumcision; the Presentation in the Temple; the growth in universal favor and sweet submission.—*Farrar*. And it is Luke who preserves the one story of the visit to the temple of Jesus at twelve years old, which is the "solitary flower gathered from the silence of thirty years."

5. Gospel of Womanhood.—Luke very prominently records the graciousness and tenderness of Christ toward childhood and womanhood. It is Luke only that tells that the young man who was raised to life at the gate of the city of Nain was the "only son of his mother, and she was a widow" (7: 11). It is Luke only who tells us that the daughter of Jairus, whom Christ restored to life, was the only daughter (8: 42). It is Luke from whom we learn that the boy who was a demoniac, whom Christ healed at the foot of Mt. Hermon after the transfiguration, was an only child (9: 38). Luke says that the children who were brought to Jesus were babes (18: 15).

6. The Gospel of Thanksgiving.—The Gospel of the Saviour begins with hymns and ends with praise; and as the thanksgivings of the meek are recorded in the first chapter, so in the last we listen to the gratitude of the faithful.—*Westcott.* At least seven times mention is made of "glorifying God" by the utterance of gratitude and praise (2: 20; 5: 25; 7: 16; 13: 13; 17: 15; 18: 43; 23: 47).

> Thou hast an ear for angel songs,
> A breath the gospel trump to fill,
> And taught by thee the church prolongs
> Her hymns of high thanksgiving still.
>
> —*Keble.*

7. The Gospel of Prayer.—This Gospel alone preserves to us the fact that our Lord was praying.

(1) When he was transfigured.

"And as he was praying, the fashion of his countenance was altered, and his raiment became white and dazzling" (Luke 9 : 29).

(2) At the baptism when the Holy Spirit descended on him.

"Now it came to pass, when all the people were baptized, that, Jesus also having been baptized, and praying, the heaven was opened, and the Holy Spirit descended in a bodily form, as a dove, upon him, and a voice came out of heaven, Thou art my beloved Son; in thee I am well pleased" (Luke 3 : 21, 22).

(3) After cleansing the leper.

"But he withdrew himself in the deserts, and prayed" (5 : 16).

(4) Before calling the twelve.

"And it came to pass in these days, that he went out into the mountain to pray; and he continued all night in prayer to God" (6 : 12).

(5) On the cross for the murderers.

"And Jesus said, Father, forgive them; for they know not what they do" (23:34).

(6) With his last breath.

"And Jesus, crying with a loud voice, said, Father, into thy hands I commend my spirit; and having said this, he gave up the ghost" (23:46).

Luke, like Paul, insists on the duty of unceasing prayer. He emphasizes this instruction by alone recording the two parables which encourage us to be intensely persistent and continuously faithful in our prayers (11: 5-13; 18: 1-8).

TOPICS FOR HOME STUDY AND CLASS DISCUSSION

1. Name and describe one miracle peculiar to Luke.
2. Name and describe one parable peculiar to Luke.
3. What probably was Luke's native city?
4. How many times, and where, is Luke mentioned in the New Testament?
5. When and under what circumstances does Luke first join Paul?
6. Name two characteristics of Luke's Gospel.
7. What was Luke's nationality? Give reasons for so thinking.

RAPID-FIRE DRILL

Use Questions 51 to 67, inclusive, in the back of this book.

BLACKBOARD OUTLINE

I. THE AUTHOR.	II. CHARACTERISTICS OF GOSPEL.
1. His Name.	1. Gos. of Sym.
2. Ear. Life.	2. Sam. Gos.
3. Prof.	3. Emph. Perean Min.
4. Nation.	4. Rev. Sac. of Inf.
5. Rela. to Paul.	5. Gos. of Wom.
6. Date of Gos.	6. Gos. of Thanks.
	7. Gos. of Prayer.

LESSON V.

The Christ of the New Testament Church According to John

I. THE AUTHOR

1. His Name.—It is generally accepted that John the apostle has written the fourth Gospel. In speaking of the Gospel, it will be recalled that three Johns were mentioned: John, the apostle, a son of Zebedee, and the brother of James, who suffered martyrdom under Herod Agrippa I.; John the Baptist, and John Mark, the author of the second Gospel.

2. His Occupation.—John was a fisherman on the Lake of Galilee (Mark 1: 19, 20).

3. His Character.—The apostle John was so faithful and thoughtful and consecrated in his discipleship that he has the memorable distinction of being called "the apostle whom Jesus loved." Nothing stronger than this can be said concerning his character. He ever followed his Master Teacher with a full, absorbing and unwavering devotion.

4. His Relation to the Other Apostles.—Peter,

James and John are with Christ when none else are,
as at the raising of Jairus' daughter (Mark 5: 37),
in the glory of the transfiguration (Matt. 17:1), and
in the agony in Gethsemane (Matt. 26: 37; Mark 14:
33). John and James were called Boanerges (sons
of thunder), implying a zeal and intensity of dis-
position which is one of the elements that go to
make up the life of a great man (Mark 3: 17). At
the time of the betrayal, Peter and John, after the
momentary confusion, followed Jesus afar off, while
the others hastened to seek safety in flight (John
18: 5). John goes on into the council chamber, while
Peter stays outside with Christ's enemies (John 18:
16, 19, 28). At the cross, John, who had been to
Christ as a brother, has left to him a brother's duty
(John 19: 26, 27). After the resurrection it is to
Peter and John that Mary Magdalene first runs with
the tidings of the empty tomb (John 20: 2); and
they were the first to go together to see what the
strange words meant. After the ascension John, of
course, was present on the day of Pentecost, and
later he, with Peter, enters the temple as a worshiper
(Acts 3: 1) and makes strong protests against the
threats of the Sanhedrin (Acts 4: 13). John is permitted to live many years after the other apostles
have died a martyr's death. It was left to him to
write five of the books of the New Testament—his
Gospel, which we are now considering, three Epistles, and the Book of Revelation.

5. The Date of the Book.—The Gospel according
to John was probably written between 85 and 90
A. D., in the city of Ephesus.

II. CHARACTERISTICS

1. John's Gospel Differs Widely from the Others. —The Gospels of Matthew, Mark and Luke are so much alike that they are styled the "synoptics"—that is, taking the *same view*. John has, however, carefully avoided repeating what others have written, and the result is that he has very few events in common with them, and when he does record things given by others, he gives details which they have omitted. This is accounted for by the fact that he wrote much later than the other Gospel writers, and cared not to repeat what they had already presented.

2. John's Gospel is Chronological.—When we count the feasts of the Jews which Christ attended, all of which are mentioned by John, we find that there were three years from the visit made to Jerusalem in the second chapter to the one at the time of his crucifixion. If we knew how long it was from his baptism until his first visit to the feast at Jerusalem, we could know definitely the duration of his ministry, but on this point the chronology is not good. It is regarded that Christ's ministry extended over a period of about three years and three months.

3. John Emphasizes the Judean Ministry.—We see how in our last study Luke laid emphasis upon the Perean ministry, which occupied the larger part of the last three months of Christ's life. By a study of the fourth Gospel we see that John has placed much emphasis upon Christ's Judean ministry, which occupied the larger part of the first year following his baptism. For the events of the first year of Christ's ministry, read the first four chapters in John's Gospel.

4. John's Gospel is a Gospel of Symbolism.—Not merely does John's Gospel contain the three great allegories of the Sheepfold, the Good Shepherd, and the Vine, from which Christian art has drawn its symbolism from the very earliest times; but the whole Gospel from end to end is penetrated with the spirit of symbolical representation. In nothing is this more apparent than in the eight miracles which the evangelist has selected for the illustration of the divine epic. His own word for them leads us to expect this: to him they are not so much miracles as "signs." The first two are introductory, and seem to be pointed out as such by John (2:11; 4:54). The turning of the water into wine exhibits the Messiah's sovereign power over inanimate matter, the healing of the official's son, his power over the noblest of living bodies. Moreover, they teach two great lessons which lie at the very root of Christianity: (1) that Christ's presence hallows the commonest events and turns the meanest elements into the richest; (2) that the way to win blessings is to trust the Bestower of them. The third sign, healing the paralytic, shows the Messiah as the great Bestower, repairing the physical as well as the spiritual ravages of sin (v. 14). In the feeding of the five thousand the Christ appears as the Support of life, in the walking on the sea as the Guardian and Guide of his followers. The giving of sight to the man born blind and the raising of Lazarus show that he is the Source of life and light to men. The last sign, wrought by the risen Christ, sums up and concludes the whole series (21: 1-12). Fallen man, restored, fed, guided, enlightened, delivered from the terrors of death, passes to the everlasting shore of peace, where the Lord is waiting to receive him.—*Plummer.*

5. **John's Gospel is a Spiritual Gospel.**—Considering this Gospel as a whole, possibly no fitter epithet can be found than that of Clement of Alexandria at the close of the second century; namely, *"the spiritual Gospel,"* which represents Christ in his work, not with special reference to the *past* (as with Matthew), or the *present* (as with Mark), or the *future* (as with Luke), but with general reference to *eternity,* in which the past, present and future are all included. In calling this the spiritual Gospel, we might make a contrast by designating the other Gospels *bodily* Gospels; that is, Matthew, Mark and Luke have much to say about what Christ did, where he went, how he acted, but John lays more emphasis upon the spiritual side. The keynote of the Gospel is Jesus, the divine One who became flesh and dwelt among us. John's great theme is set forth in his introduction (1: 1-18), which strikes the keynote of the whole Gospel.

6. **Written by an Eye-witness.**—*John's Gospel impresses one as having been written by one who was in the "inner circle."* "This is the disciple," writes the author, "that beareth witness of these things, and wrote these things: and we know that his witness is true" (John 21: 24). In the description of the various scenes in the "upper room" the Lord's

Supper was instituted. We are told that there "was at the table reclining in Jesus' bosom one of his disciples whom Jesus loved" (13: 23). In the author's description of the feeding of the five thousand, he tells about Jesus putting the question to Philip, "Whence are we to buy bread that these may eat?" and adds that he said this to prove him, for Christ himself knew what he would do. The author of this fourth Gospel seemed to know the very inner thoughts of the Master (22: 2; 21: 7; 1: 35-51; 2: 11, 17, 22; 4: 6, 8, 27; 6: 5, 8, 68-71; 9: 2; 11: 16; 12: 21).

7. A Summary of Characteristics and Coincidences.—Dr. Westcott, in his introduction to the "Study of the Gospels," gives the following table, showing the peculiarities and coincidences of the Gospel writers. The total contents of the several Gospels in this table are presented by 100.

GOSPEL.	PECULIARITIES.	COINCIDENCES.
Mark	7	93
Matthew	42	58
Luke	59	41
John	92	8

TOPICS FOR HOME STUDY AND CLASS DISCUSSION

1. Make one comparison of the four Gospels.

2. The position of the apostle John among the twelve.

3. Why Christ's mother was given into the care of the apostle John.

4. Why John omits many things told by Matthew, Mark and Luke.

5. Why John emphasizes the Judean ministry.

6. Why John is called the apostle whom Jesus loved.

7. Does John mention his own name in his Gospel?

8. The appropriateness of calling John's book the "spiritual" Gospel.

RAPID-FIRE DRILL

Use Questions 68 to 85 inclusive, in the back of this book.

BLACKBOARD OUTLINE

I. THE AUTHOR.	II. CHARACTERISTICS OF BOOK.
1. His Name.	1. Dif. Wid. from Others.
2. His Oc.	2. Chronological.
3. His Char.	3. Emph. Jud. Min.
4. His Rela. to Oth. Apos.	4. Gos. of Symp.
5. Date of Bk.	5. Spir. Gos.
	6. Writ. by Eye-wit.

LESSON VI.

Early History of the New Testament Church

A STUDY OF THE BOOK OF ACTS

The Book of Acts comes naturally after the four Gospels. While the Gospels are written to prove that Jesus is the Christ, the Son of God, and the Saviour of the world, the Book of Acts tells how the learned and the unlearned, the peasant and the king, may accept and follow Christ. It is the book of the New Testament to which all people should be referred when they want to know how to become Christians.

I. ITS AUTHOR

The Gospel according to Luke and the Book of Acts are dedicated to the same man. It is generally held that these two books were written by the same person, and this is strongly confirmed by the uniformity of style which pervades them. All the evidences, therefore, which tend to prove that Luke wrote the third book of the New Testament, have equal force in proving that he wrote the Book of Acts.

1. Some Facts About the Author.

(1) The writer was an immediate *disciple of the apostles* (Luke 1: 2).

(2) He was a *Gentile Christian*. This is indicated by being referred to as one who is not "of the circumcision" (Col. 4: 11-17). Then, too, a Jewish Christian would likely not have spoken of the elders "of the Jews" (Luke 7: 3), or of a city "of the Jews" (Luke 23: 51).

(3) The writer was a *traveling companion* of the apostle *Paul* during a large part of his ministry, and was with him during his first imprisonment in Rome (Acts 28: 16). We judge this from the so-called "we" passages (Acts 16: 10-17; 20: 5-21: 18; 27: 1-28: 16).

(4) The writer was a *man of culture*. This we judge by the classic style and "his historic taste and delicacy of mind."

2. These Facts do Not Belong To:

(1) *Barnabas*, for he was a Levite.

(2) *Silas*, for he was a distinguished member of the apostolic church at Jerusalem.

(3) *Timothy*, for he was a Lycaonian. Timothy's mother was a Jewess, and his father a Greek (Acts 16: 1).

(4) It is further true that Silas, Timothy and Barnabas were all with Paul before the "we" begins (Acts 16: 10): they were not always with him when the "we" is used; and they were sometimes with him when the writer says "they."

(5) The facts mentioned above do not fit *Titus*, for he was not at Troas when the writer uses "we" (2 Cor. 2: 12, 13).

3. These Facts Fit Luke:

(1) Luke was associated with Peter and James the Lord's brother, both of whom were apostles.

(2) Paul in his letter to the Colossians ranks Luke among the Christians of Greek origin (Col. 4: 10-14).

(3) Luke was with Paul in the Roman imprisonment, as appears from salutations sent by him in the letters to the Colossians and to Philemon, both written during that imprisonment.

(4) Paul distinguishes Luke as a physician, which implies mental culture above that of an ordinary person.

For facts concerning Luke's name, his early life, his profession, his nationality and his relation to Paul, see the previous lesson on "The Christ of the New Testament Church According to Luke."

II. LUKE'S SOURCES OF INFORMATION

1. As Luke was with Paul during all of the time covered by the so-called "we" passages, his source of information was, of course, his own personal observation. Then, too, he could get direct from Paul the account of Stephen's speech and death, and concerning all the events with which Paul had to do.

2. Concerning those events with which Paul had no connection, Luke had opportunity to converse with those who had: with Philip, the evangelist, concerning the labors in Samaria, and with Peter and James the Lord's brother, for all the events in which these two men participated.

III. THE DIVISIONS OF THE BOOK

The Book of Acts divides itself naturally into four sections:

1. The Church in Jerusalem (Acts 1: 1-8: 4).

This part treats exclusively of the Jerusalem church.

2. The Church in Transition (Acts 8: 5-12: 25).

This part tells of the spread of the gospel in Judea, Samaria and the surrounding countries.

3. Paul's Preaching Tours (Acts 13: 1-21: 16).

This takes up the life of Paul from the time he was set apart for his work until his last visit to Jerusalem at the close of his third tour.

4. Paul's Imprisonment Work (Acts 21: 17-28: 30).

We have here an account of his five years' imprisonment, which occupies the latter one-fourth of the book.

IV. THE PURPOSE OF THE BOOK

That must be the main purpose of an author to which he devotes the most space and to which all other facts used sustain a subordinate relation. In studying the Book of Acts we find that most of the book is occupied in giving detailed accounts of conversions to Christ and of attempts at the same that were unsuccessful. If we should take from this book all of the records of conversions, together with the facts and incidents preparatory to and consequent upon each, we would have very little left.

1. Chapter 1 shows how the apostles were prepared for their work of *converting* men.

2. The second chapter tells of the *converting* of three thousand people.

3. The third chapter gives an account of the *conversion* of many people, followed by the arrest and trial of Peter and John, caused by these *conversions*.

4. Chapters 4-7 tell about the persecution that grew out of opposition to these *conversions*.

5. Chapters 8, 9, 10 are devoted to the *conversions* of the Samaritans, the Ethiopian eunuch, Paul and Cornelius.

6. Chapter 11 is devoted mainly to an account of the establishment of the church in Antioch through the *conversion* of the Jews and Gentiles there.

7. Chapter 12 shows the benevolence of the new *converts* and gives an account of another persecution in Jerusalem.

8. Chapters 13 and 14 record the *conversions* on Paul's first missionary tour.

9. Chapter 15 describes the controversy about circumcision, which grew out of *conversions* on Paul's first tour.

10. Chapter 16 is occupied mainly by the events leading to and immediately connected with the *conversions* of Lydia and the Philippian jailer.

11. The *conversions* in Thessalonica and Berea are recorded in chapter 17.

12. The eighteenth chapter tells of the *conversions* at Corinth, occupying a year and a half.

13. The nineteenth chapter gives many *conversions* followed by persecutions in Ephesus.

14. Chapters 20-28 tells of Paul's last journey to Jerusalem, followed by his arrest, his attempts to convert the Jerusalem mob, Felix, Festus and Agrippa, and his journey to Rome, where he puts forth great effort to convert the people in that city. Without question, then, we see that the author's chief purpose was to set forth a multitude of *conversions* under the labors of the apostles and their coworkers so that we may know how this work was accomplished. The recorded cases of *conversions* represent all classes and conditions from the peasants to the priests, from the poor to the proconsuls, from the illiterate to the intellectual, thus showing that the gospel of Christ adapts itself to all the inhabitants of the earth.

V. ITS DATE

This book is assigned by many to the date of the last circumstance mentioned in it. This circumstance is that of Paul abiding "two whole years in his own hired dwelling, and received all that went in unto him, preaching the kingdom of God, and teaching the things concerning the Lord Jesus Christ with all boldness, none forbidding him" (Acts 28: 30, 31). That the narrative here closes without telling the reader whether Paul was liberated or put to death, leads to the conclusion that neither had taken place when the last words of this book were written.

This claim is "greatly strengthened when we consider it in connection with the course of the narrative in the last four chapters. In chapter 25 the writer gives the account of Paul's appeal to Cæsar, which broke off his trial before Festus, and which led to all the subsequent proceedings. It was in consequence of this appeal that Festus, being puzzled as to what report he should send to the emperor with the prisoner, brought his case to the attention of Agrippa, and also brought Paul himself before this young king (Acts 25: 12, 26, 27). He was sent upon the voyage described in the twenty-seventh chapter, in compliance with the law governing the right of appeal: he was cheered when life was despaired of in the storm by the divine message, 'Fear not, Paul: thou must stand before Cæsar' (22: 24); his appeal to Cæsar was the topic of the first conversation which he held with the Jews in the city of Rome (28: 17-19); and he was kept in prison two whole years awaiting his trial. Now, if his trial before Cæsar had taken place when this book was completed, whether it resulted in acquittal or conviction, it is unaccountable that the book was closed without a word on the subject. This would have been, not a mere omis-

sion, like many others which we know to have occurred in the course of the narrative—the omission
of matters the mention of which was not required by
the historical context—but the omission of the cul-
minating fact to which a long series of events pre-
viously mentioned led forward, and concerning which
the writer had deliberately awakened the curiosity
of his reader. It would be like a drama in which
the deepest interest in the sequel of the plot is excited, but which closes just at the point when the
sequel would have been the next and the last thing
to be witnessed. Or, more pointedly still, it would
be like the story of a noted trial, which would give
the arrest of the prisoner, his transportation from
a distant country to the place of trial, the incidents
of a long imprisonment leading up to the very day
of the trial, and then closing without a word about
the trial itself. Such a narrative was never written, unless it were some fictitious story thus closing
for the very purpose of tantalizing its readers. Such
a close to a serious and truthful history is unheard
of" (*McGarvey*). The natural inference then is that
Luke wrote the last of his book just at the end of
the close of the two whole years which he mentions.
This would make the date about A. D. 63.

VI. CHARACTERISTICS OF THE BOOK

1. **A Continuation of the Gospel According to
Luke.**—In the Book of Acts, Luke introduces his
work as a continuation of previous history. What
Jesus began to do and to teach, he now goes on to
do and to teach (Acts 1: 1).

2. A Great Missionary Book.—The Book of Acts tells about the preaching of the gospel to the "uttermost parts," as well as in Jerusalem, Judea and Samaria. This book shows how the gospel was "put to the test" and proven to be the power of God unto salvation.

3. A Manual of Church History.—Dr. Schaff has well said, "The Book of Acts is the best as well as the first manual of church history." It tells of the beginning of the church, of the emancipation of Christianity from Judaism, and of its various trials and triumphs during its first thirty years.

4. A Gospel of the Holy Spirit.—Dr. Plumptre suggestively calls the Book of Acts the "Gospel of the Holy Spirit." In bringing about the conversions and directing the labors recorded in the Book of Acts, the Holy Spirit is the principal actor. It is "undoubtedly a secondary, if not a co-ordinate purpose with the author, to show how this divine power was exerted in compliance with the oft-repeated promise of our Lord." The main body of the book opens with an account of the descent of the Holy Spirit, and from the first to the last it sets forth the work of the apostles and their colaborers as being ever directed by the Spirit who dwelt within them.

5. The Book Hinges Around Peter and Paul.—In the events preceding the *conversion* of Paul, Peter is the leader. It is very natural that he should figure prominently in that part of the narrative, as he was the one who was given the "keys of the kingdom" (Matt. 16: 19), and was thus to be the leader at the beginning and during the early experiences of the church. Peter, through the conversion of Cornelius, opens the door of the church to the Gentile world. Following this he drops back in the standpoint of leadership, and Paul comes forward as the chosen apostle to the Gentile people.

"Peter, among his own people, in the presence of a mixed, and, at first, in a great part unsympathetic, audience, before authorities bent on suppressing his testimony, and armed with full power for his destruction, preaching, working, anxiously meditating, drawn onward to new developments, at first reluctantly, with mental struggles and perplexity, but, when once convinced, acting promptly and decisively, meeting persecution unto the death fearlessly, candid in estimating the conduct, generous in supporting the position of an apostle in whom a common man would have recognized an opponent and a rival. Paul, standing on the same level of nobleness, but gifted with transcendent mental powers, with passions both before and after conversion far more easily excited, called on to bear witness to truth once hated before the representatives of all that was evil or prejudiced, ignorant or haughtily intellectual, sensual or arrogant, ignoble or noble, in the ancient world: on all circumstances showing the same fundamental character, stern, zealous, unshakable, but adapting himself to all circumstances with a versatility and power of adaptation so marvelous as to have supplied cavaliers with their most effective weapons of assault, but such as supply candid and earnest students with materials for realizing a character unrivaled in its influence upon all regions of spiritual life and thought."

6. This Book Shows the Value of Persecutions.—
As the direct result of the preaching of Stephen, the
first persecution broke out. Stephen himself was the
first Christian martyr. His blood was indeed the seed
of the church. Following soon after Stephen's death
the second persecution broke out, when James, the
brother of John, was beheaded by Herod (Acts 12:
1, 2), and when Peter was imprisoned and miraculously delivered (Acts 12: 3-19). The wind of persecution carried the seed of the gospel into all lands.
See Acts 5: 17-33; 7: 54-60; 8: 1-5.

7. Christianity Often Spoken of as "The Way."
—Christianity soon came to be looked upon as a
mode of life, and not simply a theory or philosophy
or creed. Christianity was called "The Way." Saul,
the pitiless persecutor, went down to Damascus determined "that if he found any that were of *the Way*,
whether men or women, he might bring them bound
to Jerusalem" (Acts 9: 2). When Paul was preaching in Ephesus he says that some people spoke evil
of "The Way" (Acts 19: 9). See also in this connection Acts 19: 23; 22: 4; 24: 22.

8. A World-wide Religion.—In the Book of Acts
we learn that Christianity, instead of being a Jewish sect, becomes a world-wide religion. "Limited
views of God's mercy melted away as the scope and
spirit of Christianity became understood."

9. The Book of Conversions.—The most evident
characteristic of the Book of Acts is expressed by
the one word *conversion*. The reader will feel this
more keenly by looking up the following records of
conversions:

(1) Three thousand on the day of Pentecost (2: 36-47).

(2) The Samaritans (8: 12).

(3) The Ethiopian eunuch (8: 27-40).

(4) Saul of Tarsus (9: 1-19).

(5) Cornelius and his household (10: 1-48).

(6) Lydia (16: 14-16).

(7) The jailer at Philippi (16: 25-34).

TOPICS FOR HOME STUDY AND CLASS DISCUSSION

1. Reasons for believing the Book of Acts to have been written by Luke.

2. The relation of Luke to Paul.

3. The sources of Luke's information.

4. The divisions of the Book of Acts.

5. Give the purpose of the book.

6. The relation of the third Gospel and the Book of Acts.

7. The appropriateness of calling Acts the "Gospel of the Holy Spirit."

8. Two men that figure most largely in this book.

9. Name two good results of persecution.

10. The appropriateness of calling Christianity "The Way."

11. Why do we call Acts the "Book of Conversions"?

RAPID-FIRE DRILL

Use Questions 86 to 92, inclusive, in the back of this book.

BLACKBOARD OUTLINE

THE PURPOSE: TO SHOW HOW TO WIN SOULS
FOR CHRIST.

Facts About the Author
{
1. Disc. of Apos.
2. Gen. Chris.
3. Comp. of Paul.
4. Man of Culture.
}

These fit Luke.

They do not fit Barnabas, Silas, Timothy, Titus.

Sources
{
1. Paul.
2. Phil. the evang. and others.
}

Divisions
{
1. Ch. in Jerus.
2. Ch. in Trans.
3. Paul's Pre. Tours.
4. Paul's Impris. Wo.
}

Characteristics
{
1. Cont. Gos. Ac. to Luke.
2. Gre. Miss. Bk.
3. Man. Ch. Hist.
4. Gos. Ho. Spi.
5. Bk. Hi. Ar. Pe. and Pa.
6. Sho. Val. Pers.
7. Chris. Spo. "The Way."
8. W-w. Religion.
9. Bk. Conv.
}

LESSON VII.

Review

In the Review, use Questions 1-92 inclusive, in the back of this book.

LESSON VIII.

The New Testament Church and the Name

I. SCRIPTURAL NAMES

1. Individual Believers were Called:

(1) *Disciples.* The word means a learner.

"If any man cometh to me and hateth not his own father, and mother, and wife, and children, and brethren, and sisters, yea, and his own life also, he can not be my disciple" (Luke 14:26).

"And as they were eating, Jesus took bread, and blessed, and brake it: and he gave to the disciples, and said, Take, eat: this is my body" (Matt. 26:26).

(2) *Brethren.* This term has reference to the fraternal relationship among the disciples.

"But be not ye called Rabbi: for one is your teacher, and all ye are brethren" (Matt. 23:8).

"This saying therefore went forth among the brethren, that that disciple should not die" (John 21:23).

(3) *Christians.* This term, of course, is derived from the word *Christ.*

"And it came to pass that even for a whole year they were gathered together with the church, and taught much people; and that the disciples were called Christians first in Antioch" (Acts 11:26).

"And Agrippa said unto Paul, With but little persuasion thou wouldest fain make me a Christian" (Acts 26:28).

"But if a man suffer as a Christian, let him not be ashamed: but let him glorify God in this name" (1 Pet. 4:16).

2. An Organization of Disciples was Called:

(1) *A Church.* The word means "the called out," with "from the world" implied.

"And I also say unto thee, that thou art Peter, and upon this rock I will build my church; and the gates of Hades shall not prevail against it" (Matt. 16:18).

(2) *Churches of Christ.*

"Salute one another with a holy kiss. All the churches of Christ salute you" (Rom. 16:16).

(3) *Church of God.*

"Unto the church of God which is at Corinth, even them that are sanctified in Christ Jesus, called to be saints, with all that call upon the name of our Lord Jesus Christ in every place, their Lord and ours" (1 Cor. 1:2).

(4) *Church of the Lord.*

"Take heed unto yourselves, and to all the flock which he purchased with his own blood" (Acts 20:28).

3. Jesus Speaks of the Church as "My" Church:

"Upon this rock I will build my church" (Matt. 16:18).

Repentance and remission of sins are to be preached in Christ's name.

"And that repentance and remission of sins should be preached in his name unto all the nations, beginning from Jerusalem" (Luke 24:47).

4. Believers are to be Baptized in Christ's Name.

"And Peter said unto them, Repent ye, and be baptized every one of you in the name of Jesus Christ unto the remission of your sins; and ye shall receive the gift of the Holy Spirit" (Acts 2:38).

5. Salvation is in His Name.

"And in none other is there salvation: for neither is there any other name under heaven, that is given among men, wherein we must be saved" (Acts 4:12).

II. THE HARM OF WEARING OTHER THAN SCRIPTURAL NAMES

1. Party Names are Contrary to Scripture.

"Now this I mean, that each one of you saith, I am of Paul; and I of Apollos; and I of Cephas; and I of Christ" (1 Cor. 1:12).

In this passage Paul chides the Christians at Corinth for wearing other names than that of Christ.

We must remember that it is possible to use the name "Christian" is a sectarian way. This spirit is also condemned by the apostle.

2. Party Names Make and Perpetuate Divisions. —Party names serve to create and perpetuate divisions in the church. Divisions are wrong, and anything that tends to foster them is wrong and should be condemned. These different names form a serious obstacle to Christian union. A great many people do not know the doctrines that separate one church from another, but they do know the names are different and they do not want to give them up.

Recently a soliciting committee for a church-building enterprise approached a business man in a certain city in Ohio and asked him for $100. He said that he thought $100 was too small an offering for such an enterprise, and that if they would honor Christ by naming the church "Church of Christ," he would make the offering $500. They were unable to make the arrangement.

3. The Great Reformers Condemned Unscriptural Names.—The great reformers of the church, for whom many of our great churches have been named, have been foremost in condemning the practice. "I pray you," said Luther, "do not call yourselves Lutherans, but Christians. Cease to cling to these party names and distinctions." "Would to God," said Wesley, "that all sectarian names were forgotten." A distinguished preacher said before the American Board, "I have not a dollar to spare in making Congregationalists, but who would not give to mission work to make Christians?" The name "Christian" is the one name all would be willing to wear. We can not all belong to this denomination nor to that one, but we can all be simply Christians. If the Christian life makes us happier and more useful, give Christ the honor by wearing his name.

SOME REFERENCE BOOKS

Sermons, by Charles Reign Scoville, Chapter III.; *Campaigning for Christ*, by J. V. Coombs, Part II., page 49; *First Principles*, by M. M. Davis, "The Name," page 201.

TOPICS FOR HOME STUDY AND CLASS DISCUSSION

1. The significance of the word *disciple*. (Let the one who discusses this quote at least three passages of Scripture where this name is used for the followers of Christ.)

2. The significance of the word *brethren*. (Give a Scripture where the name is used in reference to the disciples of Christ.)

3. The significance of the word *Christian*, and its use in the New Testament Scriptures.

4. Is it proper to say *"disciple church"*? Why not?

5. Is it Scriptural to write the phrase "disciples of Christ" with a big D?

6. Scriptural names for the organization of the followers of Christ.

7. The religious bodies to-day that place upon their local churches unscriptural names.

8. What the Scriptures have to say concerning unscriptural names.

9. The harm of wearing unscriptural names.

10. The value of wearing Scriptural names.

RAPID-FIRE DRILL

Use Questions 93 to 107, inclusive, in back of this book.

BLACKBOARD OUTLINE

I. SCRIPTURAL NAMES.	II. UNSCRIPTURAL NAMES.
1. Ind. Believers { 1. Disciples. 2. Brethren. 3. Christians.	1. Cont. to Scrip.
2. Org. of Disc. { 1. Ch. of Ch. 2. Ch. of God. 3. Ch. of the Lord.	2. Make and Perpet. Div.
3. Jes. Sp. of Ch. as "my Ch."	3. Gr. Ref. Cond. Them.

LESSON IX.

The New Testament Church and the Creed

I. THE MEANING OF THE WORD

The word "creed" comes from the Latin *"credo,"* "I believe;" hence a man's creed is what he believes.

II. ITS IMPORTANCE

The question of *creed* is one of great importance, for the creed dominates the life. He who says it does not matter what a man believes so he lives right, is entirely ignorant of the relation of man's convictions and actions. No man will rise higher than his creed. If his creed be faulty, he will imi-tate its faults. If his creed be perfect, he will ever be nearing perfection.

III. CHRIST THE CREED

The Christian's creed, the one thing all are asked to believe, and about which there is to be no differ-ence of opinion, is found in the Bible. Concerning other truths, great liberty of opinion is allowed, but concerning this there is to be no diversity of belief. It is the point where the Christian and the non-Christian separate. Peter gives voice to this creed in reply to the Lord's question at Cæsarea Philippi: "Whom say ye that I am?" (Matt. 16: 15). Peter re-plies, "Thou art the Christ, the Son of the living God." This is indeed the creed of the Christian Church. "Other foundation can no man lay than that which is laid, which is Jesus Christ" (1 Cor. 3: 11). Those who would lay other foundations, such as the Nicene Creed, the Westminster Confes-sion of Faith, or the Discipline, threaten the ruin of the superstructure. In summing up the purpose of the fourth Gospel, we have these words: "Many other signs therefore did Jesus in the presence of the disciples, which are not written in this book: but these are written that ye may believe that Jesus is the Christ, the Son of God: and that believing ye may have life in his name" (John 20: 30, 31). Again, Paul, the bearer of the gospel to the Gentiles, says, "I determined not to know anything among you, save Jesus Christ, and him crucified" (1 Cor. 2: 2). Thus in all the Bible it is not, "Do you believe in this human creed or in that confession of faith?" but, "Do you believe that Jesus is the Christ, the Son of God?" If a man preaches Jesus, he preaches the faith. If he does not preach Jesus, he does not preach the faith; hence that person whom we must preach and that one in whom we must believe is Jesus Christ—*he is the creed of the New Testament church.*

IV. THE GREATNESS OF THIS CREED

1. This Creed is Simple.—The youth, as soon as he is old enough to know right from wrong, can know Him and love Him. The uneducated can accept Him and trust Him.

2. This Creed is Profound.—He is master of masters. The deepest mind can not fathom its depth.

3. This Creed is Comprehensive.—It includes the great truths concerning God, his relation to man, and man's relation to man.

4. This Creed is Divine.—It is God manifest in the flesh. This meets the inherent demands of the soul.

5. This Creed is a Pattern.—Christ is our ideal. We become like the things we worship.

6. This Creed is Capable of Bringing Out the Best There is in Our Lives.—Under Christ's influence the best lives are developed, the greatest joys realized, and the highest destiny secured.

7. This Creed is Universal.—All admit that, whatever we preach, we, as Christians, must preach Jesus

Christ. He will attract the scientific mind as well as the imaginative and practical. We are on common ground when we kneel at his feet.

8. This Creed is Perfect.—It is one that needs no revision. It has been held over the blaze of criticism, but no flaws have been found. The highest intellects can suggest no improvements. Pilate's answer is universal: "I find no fault in him."

A word to you, dear reader: Can Christ find any unacknowledged faults in you?

TOPICS FOR DISCUSSION

1. The relation of a man's creed and his actions.

2. Discuss the statement so often heard, "It matters not what a man believes, so he lives right."

3. The creed of the New Testament church.

4. How human creeds have grown up.

5. How human creeds have retarded the progress of the church.

6. The disuse of human creeds to-day, giving reasons for the same.

7. The great value of having a personality as a creed rather than a man-made statement of faith.

8. The so-called "Apostles' Creed;" why it can not be the creed of the New Testament church.

RAPID-FIRE DRILL

Use Questions 108 to 112, inclusive, in the back of this book.

SOME REFERENCE BOOKS

The Great Salvation, by E. V. Zollars, Chapter II. of Appendix; *Campaigning for Christ*, by J. V.

Coombs, Part II., page 47; *From Darkness to Light*,
by various authors, "From Man-made Creeds to the
God-given Creed," pages 107-9.

BLACKBOARD OUTLINE

```
I.  MEANING OF WORD.        II.  ITS IMPORTANCE.
            III.  CHRIST THE CREED.
        IV.  THE GREATNESS OF THIS CREED.
    1. Simple.    2. Profound.    3. Comprehensive.
    4. Divine.    5. Pattern.     6. Br. out be. in lives.
    7. Universal. 8. Perfect.
```

LESSON X.

The New Testament Church and Conversion

I. PRESENT CONFUSION ON THE SUBJECT

1. Cause of the Confusion.—There is considerable
confusion in the minds of many Christians on this
subject. Not many, we fear, would be able to define
conversion intelligently. Surely an experience so vital to the Christian life and essential to salvation,
should be easily understood. The present confusion
is due to labored efforts to explain this change in
a person's life. It is simple enough if the Bible be
allowed to speak for itself.

2. Conversion Not Miraculous.—An effort has
been made to surround conversion with considerable mystery and supernaturalism. When the facts
are considered, the experience will be found analo-

gous to many other experiences of our common life. Conversion is not miraculous. It is not something done for us or upon us in some mysterious way. We shall presently see that all the steps in conversion are to be taken, and must be taken, by the individual himself. It is not something done for him, but something he does for himself.

3. What Conversion is Not.—Conversion is not necessarily emotional. "Feeling" is no essential part of conversion. There are many people waiting for some peculiar "feeling" as evidence of conversion. Others have experienced feelings and have taken them as evidence of conversion, who are very far from the kingdom. The fallacy lies just here, a peculiar emotional experience is no *essential* part of conversion.

II. MEANING OF CONVERSION

1. Explained by the Scripture.—The Revised Version saves us the trouble of explaining the word "convert."

"Repent ye therefore, and turn again, that your sins may be blotted out, that so there may come seasons of refreshing from the presence of the Lord" (Acts 3 : 19).

In King James' Version we have "be converted;" in the Revised Version we have "turn again." The word is almost equivalent to our expression, "Right about face." Can anything be plainer than that? Is your face and life turned away from God, then turn toward him; that is conversion.

2. The Steps.—The steps in conversion have sometimes been described as follows:

(1) *A change of mind.* Having once disbelieved, the individual, by hearing or reading the Word, changes his mind and believes.

(2) *A change of will.* Having loved the things of this world, the sinner determines or wills to transfer his affections to spiritual things. This change of will is called *repentance*. Belief in Jesus and repentance is made known by confession. The prodigal said, "I will arise and go to my father."

(3) *A change of state.* Formerly being dead in sin, the individual is now quickened by faith in and repentance toward Christ. This change is beautifully symbolized by baptism.

(4) The result is a change of life. The whole life is changed, converted, turned again. The fruits of the life are indications of this change.

"By their fruits ye shall know them. Do men gather grapes of thorns or figs of thistles?" (Matt. 7:16).
"But the fruit of the Spirit is love, joy, peace, long-suffering, kindness, goodness, faithfullness, meekness, self-control; against such there is no law" (Gal. 5:22, 23).

III. SCRIPTURE CASES OF CONVERSION

Keeping in mind the foregoing suggestions, students are requested to study carefully the following cases of conversion with the aid of the analysis. The first reference is the great commission.

NEW TESTAMENT RECORDS OF CONVERSION

Hearing	Faith	Repentance	Baptism	Results	Reference
Preaching	Faith		Baptized	Saved	Mark 16:16
Heard		Repented	Baptized	{ Sin forgiven } { H. S. received }	Acts 2:38
Heard		Repented			Acts 3:19
Heard	Faith		Baptized		Acts 8:12, 13
Heard	Faith		Baptized		Acts 8:26-39
Heard			Baptized		Acts 9:1 ff
Heard			Baptized		Acts 10:47
Heard			Baptized		Acts 16:15
Heard	Faith		Baptized		Acts 16:22-34
Heard	Faith		Baptized		Acts 18:8

SOME REFERENCE BOOKS

First Principles, by M. M. Davis, Chapters VII., VIII., IX., XI.; *Campaigning for Christ*, by J. V. Coombs, "Confession," page 48; "Repentance," page 167, and "What Must I Do to be Saved?" page 164; *Sermons*, by Charles Reign Scoville, Chapter VII.; *The Gospel Preacher*, by Benjamin Franklin, Vol. I., Sermons II., VI., XIV.; Vol. II., Sermon IV; *Seeking the Old Paths*, by Robert Moffett, Chapters XII., XIV. and XV.; *The Great Salvation*, by E. V. Zollars, Chapters VI., VII. and VIII.; *From Darkness to Light*, by various authors, "How Does a Man Get Religion?" page 34; "The Confusion Brought About by the Mourner's Bench," page 32; "The Unscripturalness of 'Roman Catholicism,'" pages 79-88; "The Story of How I Came to Christ," pages 113-120; "The Value of Having a Definite Answer when One Wants to be a Christian," pages 197-203.

TOPICS FOR HOME STUDY AND CLASS DISCUSSION

1. Why there is so much confusion concerning conversion.

2. How may a man know that he is converted?

3. What does the word "convert" mean?

4. Give a description of the conversion of the three thousand on the day of Pentecost (Acts 2: 14-42).

5. Give an account of the conversion of the Ethiopian eunuch (Acts 8: 26-40).

6. Give an account of the conversion of Paul (Acts 9: 22, 26).

7. Name and describe the steps in conversion.

8. Discuss the "mourner's-bench" or "anxious-seat" plan.

9. Why should an invitation to accept Christ be given when each gospel message is preached?

10. The value of having definite Scriptural answers for those seeking to become Christians.

RAPID-FIRE DRILL

Use Questions 113 to 122, inclusive, in the back of this book.

BLACKBOARD OUTLINE

I. PRES. CONFUSION.	II. MEANING OF CONVERSION.
1. Cause of conf.	
2. Conv. not Mirac.	1. Ex. by Scripture.
3. What conv. is not.	2. The Steps.
III. SCRIP. CASES OF CONVERSION.	

LESSON XI.

The New Testament Church and Baptism

There are two ordinances observed by the New Testament church—baptism and the Lord's Supper. The former is to be observed only once by every Christian; the latter is to be observed every first day of the week.

I. THE PLACE OF CHRISTIAN BAPTISM

1. Baptism is in the Great Commission.

"Go ye therefore, and make disciples of all the nations, baptizing them into the name of the Father and of the Son and of the Holy Spirit: teaching them to observe all things whatsoever I commanded you: and lo, I am with you always, even unto the end of the world" (Matt. 28: 19, 20).

"Go ye into all the world, and preach the gospel to the whole creation. He that believeth and is baptized shall be saved; but he that disbelieveth shall be condemned" (Mark 16: 15, 16).

2. At the Close of the First Gospel Sermon Christian Baptism was Commanded.

"And Peter said unto them, Repent ye, and be baptized every one of you in the name of Jesus Christ unto the remission of your sins; and ye shall receive the gift of the Holy Spirit" (Acts 2: 38).

3. Christian Baptism is One of the Steps in Becoming a Christian.

"Repent ye, and be baptized every one of you in the name of Jesus Christ unto the remission of your sins; and ye shall receive the gift of the Holy Spirit" (Acts 2: 38).

"And Philip opened his mouth, and beginning from this scripture, preached unto him Jesus. And as they went on the way, they came unto a certain water; and the eunuch saith, Behold, *here is* water; what doth hinder me to be baptized? And he commanded the chariot to stand still: and they both went down into the water, both Philip and the eunuch; and he baptized him. And when they came up out of the water, the Spirit of the Lord caught away Philip; and the eunuch saw him no more, for he went on his way rejoicing" (Acts 8: 35-39).

"And many of the Corinthians hearing believed, and were baptized" (Acts 18: 8).

II. FORM OF THE ORDINANCE OF BAPTISM

1. Forms Not Mentioned.—The New Testament says nothing about forms of baptism.

2. The Meaning of the Word.—The Greek word *baptizo* means *to immerse, to submerge, to dip,* but no Greek scholar in any century ever translated it *to sprinkle,* or *to pour.*

3. How the Change was Made.—There was no dispute in the New Testament church about this. The change in form originated through the Roman Catholic Church, and was copied by Protestants. Read history's record.

The first law of sprinkling was obtained in the following manner: Pope Stephen II., being driven from Rome by Adolphus, King of Lombards, in 753, fled to Pepin, who, a short time before, had usurped the crown of France. While he remained there the monks of Cressy, in Brittany, consulted him, whether, in case of necessity, baptism by pouring on the head of an infant would be lawful. Stephen replied that it would, yet pouring and sprinkling were not allowed except in cases of necessity.

It was not till the year 1311 that the legislature, in a council held at Ravenna, declared immersion or sprinkling to be indifferent. In Scotland, however, sprinkling was never practiced, in ordinary cases, until after the Reformation—about the middle of the sixteenth century. From Scotland it made its way into England, in the reign of Elizabeth, but was not authorized in the Established Church. (Art. "Baptism," in Edinburgh Encyclopedia.)

Reader, do you want to follow the dictates of the Roman Catholic Church, or will you obey Christ's command and observe this ordinance as Christ Jesus has given it to us? Choose you whom you will serve—the Pope or Christ. This is not a matter of personal preference; it is a question of loyalty to Jesus the Christ, the Son of God and our Saviour.

III. PREREQUISITES OF BAPTISM

1. Faith.

"He that believeth and is baptized shall be saved; but he that disbelieveth shall be condemned" (Mark 16:16).

2. Repentance.

"Repent ye, and be baptized every one of you in the name of Jesus Christ unto the remission of your sins; and ye shall receive the gift of the Holy Spirit" (Acts 2:38).

3. Confession.

"If thou shalt confess with thy mouth Jesus as Lord, and shalt believe in thy heart that God raised him from the dead, thou shalt be saved" (Rom. 10:9).

"Whosoever shall confess that Jesus is the Son of God, God abideth in him, and he in God" (1 John 4:15).

"Every one therefore who shall confess me before men, him will I also confess before my Father who is in heaven" (Matt. 10:32).

NOTE.—Since faith, repentance and confession are prerequisites of baptism, an infant *can not* be Scripturally baptized. Aside from being impossible, it is *wrong* to even go through the form, because those who do, are doing something in the name of Jesus about which Jesus says nothing, and for which he gives neither example nor command.

IV. PURPOSE OF BAPTISM

1. Not Mere Physical Act.—Baptism, coupled with *faith* and *repentance*, is for the remission of sins. It is not a mere physical act, but is always connected with the burial and resurrection of Christ. Viewing baptism psychologically, as well as Biblically, it has a place in the Christian life. (John 3:5; Mark 16:16; Rom. 6:4, 5; 1 Pet. 3:21.)

2. Conditions of Receiving the Gift of the Holy Spirit.—After we have *believed* on Jesus Christ, *repented* of our sins, *confessed* Christ before men and *been baptized*, we have put on Christ, and then, and not until then, can we Scripturally be called Christians. Upon doing this we receive the gift of the Holy Spirit.

"Repent ye, and be baptized every one of you in the name of Jesus Christ unto the remission of your sins; and ye shall receive the gift of the Holy Spirit" (Acts 2:38).

CHRISTIAN BAPTISM.

BAPTISM REQUIRES	IMMERSION	SPRINKLING
MUCH WATER. "And John also was baptizing in Ænon near to Salim, because there was much water there: and they came, and were baptized" (John 3:23).	YES	NO
GOING DOWN INTO THE WATER. "And he commanded the chariot to stand still; and they both went down into the water, both Philip and the eunuch: and he baptized him" (Acts 8:38).	YES	NO
BURIAL. "Having been buried with him in baptism, wherein ye were also raised with him through faith in the working of God, who raised him from the dead" (Col. 2:12). "We were buried therefore with him through baptism into death" (Rom. 6:4).	YES	NO
RESURRECTION. "As Christ was raised from the dead through the glory of the Father, so we also might walk in newness of life" (Rom. 6:4).	YES	NO
COMING UP OUT OF THE WATER. "And when they came up out of the water, the Spirit of the Lord caught away Philip; and the eunuch saw him no more, for he went on his way rejoicing (Acts 8:39).	YES	NO

IS YOUR BAPTISM SCRIPTURAL?

SOME REFERENCE BOOKS

A Great Cloud of Witnesses, by L. C. Wilson; *Immersion*, by John T. Christian; *On the Rock*, by David R. Dungan; *The Gospel Preacher*, by Benjamin Franklin, "The Action of Baptism," page 149, Vol. II.; *Campaigning for Christ*, by J. V. Coombs, Chapters III. and IV., Part II.; *The Great Salvation*, by E. V. Zollars, Chapter IX.; *First Principles*, by M. M. Davis, Chapters XII., XIII. and XIV.; *Commentary on Acts*, by J. W. McGarvey, Part II., Excursus A, pages 243-262; *From Darkness to Light*, by various authors, "Water Salvation," pages 25, 26.

TOPICS FOR HOME STUDY AND CLASS DISCUSSION

1. The value of ordinances.
2. Compare the form of service in the Old Testament institutions with those of the church.
3. The places of baptism and the preaching of the gospel.
4. Baptism as a direct command.
5. Why is the New Testament silent concerning so-called forms of baptism?
6. Why has there never been a serious debate on the question, "Is immersion Christian baptism?"
7. Name the prerequisites of Christian baptism.
8. What is the purpose of Christian baptism?
9. The origin of sprinkling and pouring?
10. Give reasons for so-called "infant baptism."
11. Is it possible to make too much of baptism? How?

12. Will any Christian doubt your baptism if you have been immersed? Why not?

13. Will any Christian doubt your baptism if you have been sprinkled?

14. Why is a Christian willing to risk his hope of eternity on a doubt, when he can be sure?

15. What can you say about baptism as a mere physical act?

RAPID-FIRE DRILL

Use Questions 123 to 136, inclusive, in the back of this book.

BLACKBOARD OUTLINE

I. PLACE OF CHRIST. BAPTISM.	III. PREREQUISITES.
1. Great Com.	1. Faith.
2. Com. at cl. of fi. gos. ser.	2. Repentance.
3. Step in becom. Christ.	3. Confession.
II. FORM OF ORDINANCE.	IV. PURPOSE.
1. Fo. not men.	1. Not mere phys. act.
2. Mean. of word.	2. Con. of rec. Ho. Spi.
3. How ch. was made.	

LESSON XII.

The New Testament Church and the Lord's Supper

I. THE NAMES

This ordinance has been variously called the Lord's Supper, Eucharist, Sacrament and Communion.

1. "The Lord's Supper," in honor of Him who instituted it.

2. "Eucharist," meaning thanksgiving, or an expression of gratitude.

3. "Sacrament," meaning an oath or pledge.

4. "Communion," meaning felllowship in which the two ideas of contributing and receiving mingle.

Of these terms, "The Lord's Supper" and "Communion" are the only ones used in the New Testament.

II. ITS PURPOSE

1. A Memorial.—According to Paul, Christ requested that as often as the disciples partook of the communion, that they do it in remembrance of him.

"In like manner also the cup, after supper, saying, This cup is the new covenant in my blood: this do, as often as ye drink it, in remembrance of me."

In order to comply with this request, every disciple's mind should be occupied with some words of Christ's or some scene in his life while the ordinance is being observed.

2. A Communion.

"The cup of blessing which we bless, is it not a communion of the blood of Christ? The bread which we break, is it not a communion of the body of Christ?" (1 Cor. 10:16).

It is not a communion with one another, but with Christ. The idea of fellowship is emphasized by the marginal reading of the American Revised Version. "A participation in." Evidently the thought in Paul's mind is, that in this ordinance we enter into sympathetic fellowship with Christ in all his efforts for man's salvation. It means that we accept these blessings for ourselves, and we are ready to join him in carrying them to others.

3. To Fortify Character.—In the faithful observance of this institution as a memorial and communion, Christian character is established. This certainly is the inevitable result of a constantly refreshed memory and a permanent realization of the incalculable benefits of Christ's life, death and resurrection.

By an abuse of the ordinance there were some who were sick, and some had even died in the time of Paul. It can be safely said that by the abuse of spiritual things the spiritual life is impoverished.

III. WHO ARE ELIGIBLE TO PARTAKE

1. All Christians.—Compare 1 Cor. 11: 23 and 1 Cor. 1: 1, 2.

"For I received of the Lord that which also I delivered unto you, that the Lord Jesus in the night in which he was betrayed took bread" (1 Cor. 11:23).

"Paul, called to be an apostle of Jesus Christ through the will of God, and Sosthenes our brother, unto the church of God which is at Corinth, *even* them that are sanctified in Christ Jesus, called *to be* saints, with all that call upon the name of our Lord Jesus Christ in every place, their *Lord* and ours" (1 Cor. 1:1, 2).

In the first passage Paul says: "I have received from the Lord that which I deliver unto *you*"—the persons to whom he was writing. Who were these persons? Reading the second reference, we find that they were: "The saints in Corinth, together with all who call upon the name of the Lord Jesus Christ."

2. Each Must Decide.—Each must decide for himself his right to partake. He must always take into consideration his spiritual condition. No church or council has the right to determine who shall or who

shall not partake. Every man shall prove himself
and then partake.

"But let a man prove himself, and so let him eat of the
bread, and drink of the cup" (1 Cor. 11 : 28).

3. Danger in Abuse.

"But let a man prove himself, and so let him eat of the
bread, and drink of the cup. For he that eateth and
drinketh, eateth and drinketh judgment unto himself, if
he discern not the body" (1 Cor. 11 : 28, 29).

IV. ITS FREQUENCY

1. Prominent in the Early Church.—The Lord's
Supper was a prominent part of the worship of the
early disciples.

"And they continued stedfastly in the apostles' teaching
and fellowship, in the breaking of bread and the prayers"
(Acts 2 : 42).

2. Every Lord's Day.—By comparing the following we discover that when the disciples met, it was
to partake of the Lord's Supper, and we know it
was their custom to meet every first day of the week.
In those days the supper was the main part of the
worship; the sermon was secondary.

"And upon the first day of the week, when we were
gathered together to break bread, Paul discoursed with
them, intending to depart on the morrow; and prolonged
his speech until midnight" (Acts 20 : 7).
"Now concerning the collection for the saints, as I
gave order to the churches of Galatia, so also do ye. Upon
the first day of the week let each one of you lay by him in
store, as he may prosper, that no collections be made when
I come" (1 Cor. 16 : 1, 2).

3. The Change.—For the first seven hundred
years the disciples continued to observe the ordinance weekly. John Calvin called the change "a
contrivance of the devil." John Wesley advised that
the table be spread each week.

TOPICS FOR HOME STUDY AND DISCUSSION

1. Why is the Lord's Supper so called?
2. Why is the Lord's Supper called *eucharist?*
3. Why is it called the *sacrament?*
4. Why is it called *communion?*
5. How often is the Lord's Supper to be observed?
6. How about the members of the Christian church that only observe the Lord's Supper once a month or once in two months; that is, those that have little or no excuse to stay away from the Lord's Supper week after week?
7. Who are eligible to partake of the Lord's Supper?
8. What do you mean by the phrase "close communion"?
9. What are some of the dangers in abusing the observance of the Lord's Supper?
10. Explain in your own words the significance of the ordinance.
11. What spiritual benefits may be received from the Lord's Supper?

RAPID-FIRE DRILL

Use Questions 137 to 145, inclusive, in the back of this book.

SOME REFERENCE BOOKS

Sermons, by Charles Reign Scoville, Chapter III.; *The Lord's Supper*, by John L. Brandt.

BLACKBOARD OUTLINE

I. THE NAMES.	**III. WHO ARE ELIGIBLE TO PARTAKE.**
1. The Lord's Supper.	
2. Eucharist.	1. All Christians.
3. Sacrament.	2. Ea. Mu. Decide.
4. Communion.	3. Dang. in Abuse.
II. PURPOSE.	**IV. ITS FREQUENCY.**
1. Memorial.	1. Prom. in Ea. Ch.
2. Communion.	2. Ev. Lo. Day.
3. To Fort. Char.	3. Change.

LESSON XIII.

The New Testament Church and the Holy Spirit

The term "Holy Spirit" is used in the New Testament no less than sixty-six times, and the terms "Spirit" and "Spirit of God" are frequently used. In this study we give just a few important facts. The students who wish to go more thoroughly into the subject will find all passages referring thereto in any good concordance.

I. THE HOLY SPIRIT IS A PERSON

1. The Holy Spirit is One with the Father and Son.

"Go ye therefore, and make disciples of all the nations, baptizing them into the name of the Father and of the Son and of the Holy Spirit" (Matt. 28:19).

"But the Comforter, even the Holy Spirit, whom the Father will send in my name, he shall teach you all things, and bring to your remembrance all that I said unto you" (John 14:26).

2. The Holy Spirit is a Comforter.

"And hope putteth not to shame; because the love of God hath been shed abroad in our hearts through the Holy Spirit which was given unto us" (Rom. 5:5).

"But if ye are led by the Spirit, ye are not under the law" (Gal. 5:18).

3. The Holy Spirit is a Guide.—He guided the apostles into all truth by bringing to their remembrance all that Jesus taught them, and thus brought the truth of Jesus before the minds of men.

"These things have I spoken unto you, while *yet* abiding with you. But the Comforter, *even* the Holy Spirit, whom the Father will send in my name, he shall teach you all things, and bring to your remembrance all that I said unto you" (John 14:15-26).

"Nevertheless I tell you the truth: It is expedient for you that I go away; for if I go not away, the Comforter will not come unto you; but if I go, I will send him unto you. And he, when he is come, will convict the world in respect of sin, and of righteousness, and of judgment: of sin, because they believe not on me; of righteousness, because I go to the Father, and ye behold me no more; of judgment, because the prince of this world hath been judged" (John 16:7-11).

4. The Holy Spirit May be Resisted.

"Ye stiffnecked and uncircumcised in heart and ears, ye do always resist the Holy Spirit: as your fathers did, so do ye" (Acts 7:51).

5. The Holy Spirit May be Grieved.

"And grieve not the Holy Spirit of God, in whom ye were sealed unto the day of redemption" (Eph. 4:30).

"Quench not the Spirit" (1 Thess. 5:19).

II. THREE MANIFESTATIONS OF THE HOLY SPIRIT

The baptism with the Holy Spirit, the extraordinary gift of the Holy Spirit that the apostles were able to bestow, and the ordinary gift or indwelling of the Holy Spirit that we are promised from God, should be gotten clearly in mind.

1. The Baptism with the Holy Spirit.—The baptism with the Holy Spirit was a miraculous manifestation. It only occurred twice. First, on the day of Pentecost, which marks the beginning of the Christian church.

"And they were all filled with the Holy Spirit, and began to speak with other tongues, as the Spirit gave them utterance" (Acts 2:4).

The second, in the household of Cornelius, which marks the beginning of the spread of the gospel among the Gentiles.

"While Peter yet spake these words, the Holy Spirit fell on all them that heard the word. And they of the circumcision that believed were amazed, as many as came with Peter, because that on the Gentiles also was poured out the gift of the Holy Spirit. For they heard them speak with tongues, and magnify God" (Acts 10:44-46).

The manifest purpose of these miraculous manifestations was to endow the apostles for their work, and to confirm the message that they were to deliver. We are not promised the baptism with the Holy Spirit to-day.

2. The Extraordinary Gift of the Holy Spirit.— The gift of the Holy Spirit which the apostles were able to bestow was an extraordinary gift, and was different from the baptism with the Holy Spirit. The latter was from heaven, but the former was given by the laying on of hands and prayer.

"Now when the apostles that were at Jerusalem heard that Samaria had received the word of God, they sent unto them Peter and John: who, when they were come down, prayed for them, that they might receive the Holy Spirit: for as yet it was fallen upon none of them: only they had been baptized into the name of the Lord Jesus. Then they laid their hands on them, and they received the Holy Spirit" (Acts 8 : 14-17).

"And when Paul had laid his hands upon them, the Holy Spirit came on them; and they spake with tongues, and prophesied" (Acts 19 : 6).

"Neglect not the gift that is in thee, which was given thee by prophecy, with the laying on of the hands of the presbytery" (1 Tim. 4 : 14).

These gifts, sometimes called secondary gifts in comparison with the baptism with the Holy Spirit, were confined to the apostolic age.

3. The Ordinary Gift of the Holy Spirit.—The ordinary gift or indwelling of the Holy Spirit that is promised to each Christian, is that which manifests itself by the fruits of the Spirit. Peter said: "Repent ye, and be baptized every one of you in the name of Jesus Christ unto the remission of your sins, and ye shall receive the gift of the Holy Spirit" (Acts 2: 38). Peter further testifies: "And we are witnesses of these things; and so is the Holy Spirit, whom God hath given to them that obey him" (Acts 5: 32). "The fruit of the Spirit is love, joy, peace, longsuffering, gentleness, goodness, faithfulness, meekness, temperance; against such there is no law" (Gal. 5: 22, 23).

III. THE OPERATION OF THE HOLY SPIRIT IS THROUGH THE WORD; *i. e.,* THE BIBLE

The Word is the effective instrument for reaching men. "The Spirit himself beareth witness with our spirit, that we are children of God" (Rom. 8: 16). This witness is borne through the Word. The Spirit says (through the Word), "Believe"; my spirit says, "I do believe." The Spirit says (through the Word),

"Repent"; my spirit says, "I have repented." The Spirit says, "Confess Christ"; my spirit says, "I have confessed him." The Spirit says, "Be baptized"; my spirit says, "I have been baptized." The Spirit says, "Live an earnest, Christlike life"; my spirit says, "I am striving to live an earnest, Christlike life." Hence the Spirit himself beareth witness with my spirit that I am a child of God, an heir of God, and a joint-heir with Christ.

TOPICS FOR HOME STUDY AND CLASS DISCUSSION

1. How does the Spirit guide us into all truth?

2. Explain the difference between the baptism with the Holy Spirit and the gift of the Holy Spirit that the apostles were able to bestow.

3. Explain the difference between the baptism with the Holy Spirit and the gift of the Holy Spirit promised to every obedient disciple?

4. How may we know that we are children of God?

5. When does a person receive the gift of the Holy Spirit?

6. What part does the Holy Spirit have in conversion?

7. Describe the Holy Spirit in so far as the Scriptures explain who he is.

RAPID-FIRE DRILL

Use Questions 146 to 149, inclusive, in the back of this book.

SOME REFERENCE BOOKS

On the Rock, by David R. Dungan, pages 199-208; *Seeking the Old Paths*, by Robert Moffett, Chapter IV.; *Campaigning for Christ*, by J. V. Coombs, Chapter VI., pages 193-6; *The Great Salvation*, by E. V. Zollars, Chapter X.; McGarvey's *Commentary on Acts*, Part I., page 39; Part II., page 142.

BLACKBOARD OUTLINE

II. HOLY SPIRIT A PERSON.	II. THREE MANIFES-TATIONS.
1. One wi. Fa. and Son.	
2. Comforter.	1. Bap. wi. Ho. Spi.
3. Guide.	2. Ex. Gi. of Ho. Spi.
4. May be Resisted.	3. Ord. Gi. of Ho. Spi.
5. May be Grieved.	
III. OPERATION IS THROUGH THE BIBLE.	

LESSON XIV.

The New Testament Church and Organization

Christ's plan is to save the world by the preaching of the gospel.

"Go ye therefore, and make disciples of all the nations, baptizing them into the name of the Father and of the Son and of the Holy Spirit; teaching them to observe all things whatsoever I commanded you: and, lo, I am with you always, even unto the end of the world" (Matt. 28 : 19, 20).

To carry out this plan there must be some organization. This organization is the church, and, as all organizations, it must have officers. This organization is simple, and is a model for all ages.

I. THE CHURCH AND ITS WORK

1. Its Purpose.—The church is a band of Christians organized for worship and work.

2. The Meaning of the Word.—The word "church" is *ekklesia* in Greek, and means "called out."

3. Power Within.—It is self-controlled, self-supported and self-extended.

4. Its Twofold Purpose.—It must win souls to Christ and train and care for those who have been won to him.

II. THE CHURCH AND THE RELATION OF ITS OFFICERS AND OTHER MEMBERS

1. No Masters and Servants.—In the church there is small distinction between the officers, which include the minister, and other members.

"Neither be ye called masters, for one is your Master, even the Christ" (Matt. 23:10).

"But we beseech you, brethren, to know them that labor among you, and are over you in the Lord, and admonish you" (1 Thess. 5:12).

2. The Measure of Success.—The distinction is that of service. By their fruits ye shall know them.

III. THE CHURCH AND ITS BEGINNING

1. On the Day of Pentecost.—The church began on the day of Pentecost following the ascension of Christ.

"They then that received his word were baptized: and there were added *unto them* in that day about three thousand souls. And they continued stedfastly in the apostles' teaching and fellowship, in the breaking of bread and the prayers" (Acts 2:41, 42).

2. Spoken of as in the Future.—In the third year of Christ's ministry he spoke of the church as in the future.

"Now when Jesus came into the parts of Cæsarea Philippi, he asked his disciples, saying, Who do men say that the Son of man is? And they said, Some *say* John the Baptist; some, Elijah; and others, Jeremiah, or one of the prophets. He saith unto them, But who say ye that I am? And Simon Peter answered and said, Thou art the Christ, the Son of the living God. And Jesus answered and said unto him, Blessed art thou, Simon Bar-Jonah: for flesh and blood hath not revealed it unto thee, but my Father who is in heaven. And I also say unto thee, that thou art Peter, and upon this rock I will build my church; and the gates of Hades shall not prevail against it. I will give unto thee the keys of the kingdom of heaven: and whatsoever thou shalt bind on earth shall be bound in heaven; and whatsoever thou shalt loose on earth shall be loosed in heaven. Then charged he the disciples that they should tell no man that he was the Christ" (Matt. 16: 13-20).

3. Spoken of as in the Past.—After Pentecost, following the resurrection, the church is spoken of as already in existence.

"And the Lord added to them day by day those that were saved" (Acts 2: 47).

IV. THE CHURCH AND ITS OFFICERS

1. Christ the Head.

"And he put all things in subjection under his feet, and gave him to be head over all things to the church" (Eph. 1: 22).

"And he is the head of the body, the church: who is the beginning, the firstborn from the dead; that in all things he might have the pre-eminence" (Col. 1: 18).

(1) *Corner-stone.*

"Because it is contained in Scripture,
    Behold, I lay in Zion a chief corner-stone, elect, precious;
    And he that believeth on him shall not be put to shame" (1 Pet. 2: 6).

(2) *Foundation.*

"For other foundation can no man lay than that which is laid, which is Jesus Christ" (1 Cor. 3 : 11).

2. Apostles.

(1) *Chosen and trained by Christ.*

"And when it was day, he called his disciples ; and he chose from them twelve, whom he also named apostles" (Luke 6 : 13).

(2) *Qualifications:* (*a*) Witnesses of the risen Saviour. (*b*) Given miraculous power.

The apostles had no successors.

3. Prophets.

They were inspired teachers.

"Now in these days there came down prophets from Jerusalem unto Antioch" (Acts 11 : 27).
"Now there were at Antioch, in the church that was *there*, prophets and teachers, Barnabas, and Symeon that was called Niger, and Lucius of Cyrene, and Manaen the foster-brother of Herod the tetrarch, and Saul. And as they ministered to the Lord, and fasted, the Holy Spirit said, Separate me Barnabas and Saul for the work whereunto I have called them" (Acts 13 : 1, 2).

The prophets had no successors. We have an inspired book as our rule of faith and practice.

4. Evangelists.

"And on the morrow we departed and came unto Cæsarea : and entering into the house of Philip the evangelist, who was one of the seven, we abode with him" (Acts 21 : 8).
"And he gave some *to be* apostles ; and some, prophets ; and some, evangelists ; and some, pastors and teachers" (Eph. 4 : 11).
"But be thou sober in all things, suffer hardship, do the work of an evangelist, fulfill thy ministry" (2 Tim. 4 : 5).

An evangelist is a bearer of good news. Every Christian is an evangelist.

5. Deacons.

(1) *Qualifications.*

"Deacons in like manner *must be* grave, not double-tongued, not given to much wine, not greedy of filthy lucre; holding the mystery of the faith in a pure conscience. And let these also first be proved; then let them serve as deacons, if they be blameless. Women in like manner *must be* grave, not slanderers, temperate, faithful in all things. Let deacons be husbands of one wife, ruling *their* children and their own houses well. For they that have served well as deacons gain to themselves a good standing, and great boldness in the faith which is in Christ Jesus" (1 Tim. 3: 8-13).

(2) *Duties:* (*a*) Serve tables (Acts 6: 2). Here we have mentioned the first deacons. (*b*) Look after the temporal welfare of the church.

"Now in these days, when the number of the disciples was multiplying, there arose a murmuring of the Grecian Jews against the Hebrews, because their widows were neglected in the daily ministration. And the twelve called the multitude of the disciples unto them, and said, It is not fit that we should forsake the word of God, and serve tables. Look ye out therefore, brethren, from among you seven men of good report, full of the Spirit and of wisdom, whom we may appoint over this business. But we will continue steadfastly in prayer, and in the ministry of the word. And the saying pleased the whole multitude: and they chose Stephen, a man full of faith and of the Holy Spirit, and Philip, and Prochorus, and Nicanor, and Timon, and Parmenas, and Nicolaus a proselyte of Antioch; whom they set before the apostles: and when they had prayed, they laid their hands upon them (Acts 6: 1-6).

(3) *Reward:* "Good standing and great boldness in the faith which is in Christ Jesus."

"For they that have served well as deacons gain to themselves a good standing, and great boldness in the faith which is in Christ Jesus" (1 Tim. 3: 13).

(4) *Meaning of Word.* The Greek word translated "deacon" signifies servant, and is so translated.

"But he that is greatest among you shall be your servant" (Matt. 23: 11).
"If any man serve me, let him follow me; and where I am, there shall also my servant be: if any man serve me, him will the Father honor" (John 12: 26).

Also translated "minister."

"But it is not so among you: but whosoever would become great among you, shall be your minister" (Mark 10:43).

"What then is Apollos? and what is Paul? Ministers through whom ye believed; and each as the Lord gave to him" (1 Cor. 3:5).

"And sent Timothy, our brother and God's minister in the gospel of Christ, to establish you, and to comfort you concerning your faith" (1 Thess. 3:2).

(5) Note also the church at Cenchreæ had a deaconess:

"I commend unto you Phœbe our sister, who is a servant of the church that is at Cenchreæ" (Rom. 16:1—R. V. margin).

6. Elders.

(1) *Other names:* Bishop, presbyter, overseer, pastor.

"And he gave some *to be* apostles; and some, prophets; and some, evangelists; and some, pastors and teachers" (Eph. 4:11).

(2) *Qualifications:*

"Faithful is the saying, If a man seeketh the office of a bishop, he desireth a good work. The bishop therefore must be without reproach, the husband of one wife, temperate, sober-minded, orderly, given to hospitality, apt to teach; no brawler, no striker; but gentle, not contentious, no lover of money; one that ruleth well his own house, having *his* children in subjection with all gravity; (but if a man knoweth not how to rule his own house, how shall he take care of the church of God?) not a novice, lest being puffed up he fall into the condemnation of the devil. Moreover he must have good testimony from them that are without; lest he fall into reproach and the snare of the devil" (1 Tim. 3:1-7).

"For this cause I left thee in Crete, that thou shouldest set in order the things that were wanting, and appoint elders in every city, as I gave thee charge; if any man is blameless, the husband of one wife, having children that believe, who are not accused of riot or unruly. For the bishop must be blameless, as God's steward; not self-willed, not soon angry, no brawler, no striker, not greedy of filthy lucre; but given to hospitality, a lover of good, sober-minded, just, holy, self-controlled; holding to the faithful word which is according to the teaching, that he may be able both to exhort in the sound doctrine, and to convict the gainsayers" (Tit. 1:5-9).

(3) *Duties:* (*a*) Watch themselves.

"Take heed unto yourselves, and to all the flock, in which the Holy Spirit hath made you bishops, to feed the church of the Lord which he purchased with his own blood" (Acts 20 : 28).

(*b*) Set a good example.

"Neither as lording it over the charge allotted to you, but making yourselves ensamples to the flock" (1 Pet. 5 : 3).

(*c*) Teach and exhort.

"Holding to the faithful word which is according to the teaching, that he may be able both to exhort in the sound doctrine, and to convict the gainsayers.
"For there are many unruly men, vain talkers and deceivers, specially they of the circumcision, whose mouths must be stopped; men who overthrow whole houses, teaching things which they ought not for filthy lucre's sake" (Tit. 1 : 9-11).

(*d*) Visit the sick.

"Is any among you sick? let him call for the elders of the church; and let them pray over him, anointing him with oil in the name of the Lord" (Jas. 5 : 14).

(*e*) Oversee the flock.

"Tend the flock of God which is among you, exercising the oversight, not of constraint, but willingly, according to *the will of God;* not yet for filthy lucre, but of a ready mind" (1 Pet. 5 : 2).
"Take heed unto yourselves, and to all the flock, in which the Holy Spirit hath made you bishops, to feed the church of the Lord which he purchased with his own blood" (Acts 20 : 28).

(4) *Reward:* Crown of Glory.

"And when the chief shepherd shall be manifested, ye shall receive the crown of glory that fadeth not away" (1 Pet. 5 : 4).

TOPICS FOR HOME STUDY AND CLASS DISCUSSION

1. What is the church?

2. Does the New Testament make any distinction between the minister and other disciples?

3. Who were the apostles? Have they any successors?

4. Who were the prophets? Have they any successors?

5. Describe the work of an evangelist.

6. Tell the qualifications and duties of a deacon.

7. Tell the qualifications and duties of an elder.

8. What other names are used to describe the office of an elder?

9. What is the modern pastor—an elder or deacon, or both?

10. Should an elder be a Bible-school teacher?

11. Who should constitute the "official board"?

RAPID-FIRE DRILL

Use Questions 150 to 155, inclusive, in the back of this book.

BLACKBOARD OUTLINE

I. CHURCH AND ITS WORK.	III. CHURCH AND ITS BEGINNING.
1. Its Pur.	1. On the Day of Pentecost.
2. Mean. of Word.	2. Spoken of as in the Future.
3. Pow. within.	2. Spoken of as in the Past.
4. Twofold Pur.	
	IV. CHURCH AND OFFICES.
II. CHURCH—RELATION OF OFF., ETC.	1. Christ, the Head
1. No. Mas. and Ser.	2. Apostles.
2. Meas. of Suc.	6. Prophets.
	4. Evangelists.
	5. Deacons.
	6. Elders.

LESSON XV.

The New Testament Church and Finances

The whole life and teachings of Jesus are filled with the spirit of giving. His unselfish life, his sacrificial death, his altruistic teachings, have given us a new conception of man, his life's work and his possessions. The Christian is taught that he is responsible to God for everything that he possesses. A Christian is never to lose sight of Christ. He must buy his clothes as a Christian. He must furnish his table as a Christian. He must buy his books as a Christian. In other words, the Christian is just as much responsible for the use of the dollar that he spends for a pair of gloves as he is for the one he gives to Foreign Missions.

1. Giving is a Duty.—It is a definite part of the Christian life.

"But as ye abound in everything, *in* faith, and utterance, and knowledge, and in all earnestness, and *in* your love to us, *see* that ye abound in this grace also" (2 Cor. 8:7).

"I beseech you therefore, brethren, by the mercies of God, to present your bodies a living sacrifice, holy, acceptable to God, which is your spiritual service" (Rom. 12:1).

"And Jesus looking upon him loved him, and saith unto him, One thing thou lackest: go sell whatsoever thou hast, and give to the poor, and thou shalt have treasure in heaven: and come, follow me" (Mark 10:21).

"Upon the first day of the week let each one of you lay by him in store, as he may prosper, that no collections be made when I come" (1 Cor. 16:2).

2. Giving is Reciprocal.—A Christian is blessed by giving.

"But this I *say*, He that soweth sparingly shall reap

also sparingly; and he that soweth bountifully shall reap also bountifully" (2 Cor. 9:6).

"Give, and it shall be given unto you; good measure, pressed down, shaken together, running over, shall they give into your bosom. For with what measure ye mete it shall be measured to you again" (Luke 6:38).

"Jesus said unto him, If thou wouldest be perfect, go sell that which thou hast, and give to the poor, and thou shalt have treasure in heaven: and come, follow me" (Matt. 19:21).

The following inscription is said to be on a tombstone in Tiverton, England:

> "That wee spent, wee had;
> That wee lefte, we loste;
> That wee gave, we have."

3. Giving is Noticed by Our Saviour.

"And he called unto him his disciples, and said unto them, Verily I say unto you, This poor widow cast in more than all they that are casting into the treasury" (Mark 12:43).

We should give as though we were placing our gifts in the pierced hands of Christ Jesus.

> 'Give as you would if an angel
> Awaited your gift at the door;
> Give as you would if to-morrow
> Found you where waiting was o'er;
> Give as you would to the Master
> If you met his searching look;
> Give as you would of your substance
> If his hand your offering took."

4. Giving Must be Cheerful.

"Let each man do according as he hath purposed in his heart: not grudgingly, or of necessity: for God loveth a cheerful giver" (2 Cor. 9:7).

5. Giving Must be Liberal.

"Or he that exhorteth, to his exhorting: he that giveth, let him do it with liberality; he that ruleth, with diligence; he that showeth mercy, with cheerfulness" (Rom. 12:8).

The Greek word translated "cheerful" in 2 Cor. 9:7, means "hilarious." In Rom. 12:8, the word "simplicity" is rendered in the Revised Version "liberality."

6. Giving Not Limited by Geographical Boundaries.—Giving must not be limited by geographical or racial boundaries. This being true, each Christian should give both to Home and Foreign Missions. The world is the Christian's field.

"And the field is the world; and the good seed, these are the sons of the kingdom: and the tares are the sons of the evil one" (Matt. 13:38).

"Go ye therefore, and make disciples of all the nations, baptizing them into the name of the Father and of the Son and of the Holy Spirit" (Matt. 28:19).

"And how shall they preach, except they be sent? even as it is written, How beautiful are the feet of them that bring glad tidings of good things" (Rom. 10:15).

"Blessed are they that wash their robes, that they may have the right to come to the tree of life, and may enter in by the gates into the city" (Rev. 22:14).

7. Giving Not Irregular.—Giving should be systematic, universal and proportionate. Upon the first day of the week let every one of you lay by him in store as he may prosper. (A. V., as God has prospered him.)

"Upon the first day of the week let each one of you lay by him in store, as he may prosper, that no collections be made when I come" (1 Cor. 16:2).

8. Money Must Not Stand Between Us and Our Saviour.

"Jesus said unto him, If thou wouldest be perfect, go, sell that which thou hast, and give to the poor, and thou shalt have treasure in heaven: and come, follow me. But when the young man heard the saying, he went away sorrowful; for he was one that had great possessions. And Jesus said unto his disciples, Verily I say unto you, It is hard for a rich man to enter into the kingdom of heaven. And again I say unto you, It is easier for a camel to go through a needle's eye, than for a rich man to enter into the kingdom of God" (Matt. 19:21-24).

Coveted money caused Judas to betray his Master.

Dives misused his money and would gladly have changed his life after it was too late. The rich young man was told to get rid of his money and come and follow his Saviour. The selfish farmer trusted too much in things temporal. Death's sentence came with the question, "The things which thou hast prepared, whose shall they be?" (Luke 12: 20.) In giving as well as living, Christ must have no secondary place.

9. Money is Potent and Far-reaching.—Money properly used is a power for good. If I rightly answer the question, "What shall I do with myself?" I can then easily answer the other, "What shall I do with my money?"

In a Japanese temple the coffer or collection-box stands at the entrance of the door. No heathen ever prays to his god till he has first given his money, or his rice or his silk. It is always *pay* first, then pray; otherwise the god would be insulted. Is there not a lesson in this for the Christian? You can not do everything, but you can help do a great many things. Dr. Dennis has well and truthfully said: "An ordinary contributor, as he sits in his pew, can touch every continent, and do a work for Christ where his footsteps can never tread." Put your very self into your gifts. Forget not that behind each gift must be the loving, praying, sympathetic heart of the giver.

> "Not what we give, but what we share,
> For the gift without the giver is bare;
> Who gives himself with his alms feeds three—
> Himself, his hungry neighbor and Me."
>
> *—Lowell.*

TRY THIS PLAN

Reader, will you not pledge a definite proportion to be given prayerfully and carefully for the work of the Lord? Are we treating the Lord right by giving him the nickels or dimes that we happen to have in our pockets when the offering-basket is passed? Will you permit the evangelization of the world to depend upon the condition of your pocket-book on the special days when the regular missionary offerings are taken? Fill out the following pledge. Try it at least for a year, and we believe you will so greatly enjoy it that you will continue. It pays. Pays in spiritual blessing. Pays in temporal blessing. Pays by giving you a higher, happier, richer Christian experience. Sign it now.

I hereby promise to give one-tenth of my income to the Lord for one year.

Date .... Name ....

TOPICS FOR HOME STUDY AND CLASS DISCUSSION

1. Discuss the reciprocity of giving.
2. Why should giving be done cheerfully?
3. Discuss the value of systematic giving.
4. Discuss the value of proportionate giving.
5. Discuss the value of the tithing system.
6. The questions confronting a rich disciple of Christ.
7. Giving as a grace (2 Cor. 8: 7).
8. The best plan for raising money for the current expenses of the church.

RAPID-FIRE DRILL

Use Questions 156 to 162, inclusive, in the back of this book.

BLACKBOARD OUTLINE

```
GIVING ⎰ A Duty.
       ⎱ Reciprocal.
         Not. by Sav.
         Mu. be Cheer.
         Mu. be Lib.
         Not Lim. by Ge. Bo.
         Giv. not Ir.
         Mo. Mu. not St. bet. Us and Sav.
         Mo. Pot. and Far-re.
```

LESSON XVI.

The New Testament Church and Missions

I. CHRIST THE GREAT MISSIONARY

1. A Definition.—A missionary is one sent with a message to another person. Christ was sent into the world, by his Father and ours, to deliver unto us a message of his love and forgiveness. Christ himself so conceived his mission.

2. The Work of the Great Missionary.—With this conception of his ministry, he was tireless in his efforts to reach as many people as possible during his lifetime.

"And it came to pass soon afterwards, that he went about through the cities and villages, preaching and bringing the good tidings of the kingdom of God, and with him the twelve" (Luke 8:1).

"The thief cometh not, but that he may steal, and kill, and destroy: I came that they may have life, and may have *it* abundantly" (John 10:10).

3. The Work of the Disciples.—The task committed to the Christ was an enormous one. It was utterly impossible for him to touch personally all human beings in his lifetime. So he deputized his disciples to assist him in this work.

"And he said unto them, Go ye into all the world, and preach the gospel to the whole creation. He that believeth and is baptized shall be saved; but he that disbelieveth shall be condemned" (Mark 16:15, 16).
"But ye shall receive power, when the Holy Spirit is come upon you: and ye shall be my witnesses both in Jerusalem, and in all Judea and Samaria, and unto the uttermost parts of the earth" (Acts 1:8).

4. The Law of Growth.—In the parable of the leaven Christ showed clearly the law of growth in his spiritual kingdom. As the leaven is passed on from atom to atom by contact, so the gospel is to be passed from person to person until the whole human race has felt the touch of Christ. If one person fails to do his part, the truth will fail to spread in his direction until he is removed and a more faithful one takes his place.

"Another parable spake he unto them: The kingdom of heaven is like unto leaven, which a woman took, and hid in three measures of meal, till it was all leavened" (Matt. 13:33).

II. THE DISCIPLES CAUGHT HIS SPIRIT

1. Zeal of Early Christians.—When scattered by persecutions they went everywhere preaching the gospel. When a church was broken up by the enemy, they scattered like brands from a fire, each starting a new fire of faith and zeal. Mark says the zeal of the early disciples carried them into all the regions of Palestine.

"And they went forth, and preached everywhere, the Lord working with them, and confirming the word by the signs that followed" (Mark 16 : 20).

2. Peter and Cornelius.—Peter was sent to Cornelius and was taught that it is God's purpose to give all an opportunity to know the truth that makes men free.

"But in every nation he that feareth him, and worketh righteousness, is acceptable to him" (Acts 10 : 35).

3. Paul in His Larger Work.—Paul hears the famous Macedonian call, and starts on his historical trip through Europe.

"And a vision appeared to Paul in the night: There was a man of Macedonia standing, beseeching him, and saying, Come over into Macedonia, and help us. And when he had seen the vision, straightway we sought to go forth into Macedonia, concluding that God had called us to preach the gospel unto them" (Acts 16 : 9, 10).

4. The Last Command.—Christ's last and great commission was, "Go therefore and make disciples of all the nations." The program to be followed is given by Luke.

"But ye shall receive power, when the Holy Spirit is come upon you: and ye shall be my witnesses both in Jerusalem, and in all Judea and Samaria, and unto the uttermost part of the earth" (Acts 1 : 8).

To those living in America, Jerusalem represents our local field; Judea, the State work; Samaria, America; the uttermost parts of the world, Foreign Missions.

The teacher should here explain the necessity for State Missionary Boards, the American Christian Missionary Society, the Foreign Christian Missionary Society, the Board of Church Extension, the

Lincoln Christian College

Board of Ministerial Relief, the National Benevolent Association, and the C. W. B. M.

III. THE CHURCHES WERE MISSIONARY

1. **Missionary Churches.**—The work of spreading the good news was not merely an individual matter and duty, but the disciples co-operated in the work. While many disciples went to do missionary work on their own responsibility and supported themselves by their hands as Paul did, we can find evidences of co-operation along missionary and benevolent lines.

2. **Offerings from Churches.**—The churches were accustomed to take offerings. It is certainly reasonable to suppose that among the purposes for which offerings were taken would be the work of evangelizing.

"Now concerning the collection for the saints, as I gave order to the churches of Galatia, so also do ye. Upon the first day of the week let each one of you lay by him in store, as he may prosper, that no collections be made when I come. And when I arrive, whomsoever ye shall approve, them will I send with letters to carry your bounty unto Jerusalem: and if it be meet for me to go also, they shall go with me" (1 Cor. 15 : 1-5).

3. **Missions the Center.**—When we talk about missions in the New Testament church, we are talking about the very genius and heart of Christ's work for men. It was the missionary spirit that brought him into the world, and that inspired all the apostles and early disciples. All Gentile nations are enjoying the fruits of missionary labor. So thoroughly are missions the mission of the Christ and his church, that one might be excused for thinking any professed disciple of his who is not missionary has failed utterly to catch the Christ spirit.

SOME REFERENCE BOOKS

Missionary Fields and Forces, by William J. Lhamon; *Seeking the Old Paths*, by Robert Moffett, Chapter VIII.

TOPICS FOR HOME STUDY AND CLASS DISCUSSION

1. Christ, the great missionary.
2. The missionary program as given by Luke.
3. The missionary spirit in the early churches.
4. How to create a missionary conscience in the church of to-day.
5. The value of State, national and world-wide missionary organizations.
6. The value of missionary organizations in the local church.
7. Paul the missionary.
8. Encouraging features of modern missionary work.

RAPID-FIRE DRILL

Use Questions 163 to 169, inclusive, in the back of this book.

BLACKBOARD OUTLINE

I. CHRIST, THE GREAT MISSIONARY.	II. DISCIPLES CAUGHT HIS SPIRIT.
1. Definition.	1. Zeal of Ear. Christ.
2. Wo. of Gr. Miss.	2. Pet. and Cor.
3. Wo. of Disc.	3. Paul in Lar. Wo.
4. Law of Growth.	4. La. Com.

III. CHURCHES WERE MISSIONARY.		
1. Miss. Ch.	2. Off. fr. Ch.	3. Miss. the Cen.

LESSON XVII.

The New Testament Church and Judgment

I. PARABLES OF THE JUDGMENT

The judgment was a frequent theme with Christ and the apostles. Christ taught the people to expect and prepare for it. One of the finest verbal pictures drawn by the Master is recorded in Matt. 25, and is a vivid picture of the judgment. The subject was not used by the Christ to frighten people. He speaks of it as he does of other great truths. The Master at one time chided the Pharisees for neglecting to consider judgment.

"But woe unto you Pharisees! for ye tithe mint and rue and every herb, and pass over justice and the love of God: but these ought ye to have done, and not to leave the other undone" (Luke 11:42).

1. Parable of the Ten Virgins.

"Then shall the kingdom of heaven be likened unto ten virgins, who took their lamps, and went forth to meet the bridegroom. And five of them were foolish, and five were wise. For the foolish, when they took their lamps, took no oil with them: but the wise took oil in their vessels with their lamps. Now while the bridegroom tarried, they all slumbered and slept. But at midnight there is a cry, Behold, the bridegroom! Come ye forth to meet him. Then all those virgins arose, and trimmed their lamps. And the foolish said unto the wise, Give us of your oil; for our lamps are going out. But the wise answered, saying, Peradventure there will not be enough for us and you: go ye rather to them that sell, and buy for yourselves. And while they went away to buy, the bridegroom came; and they that were ready went in with him to the marriage feast: and the door was shut. Afterward came also the other virgins, saying, Lord, Lord, open to us. But he answered and said, Verily I say unto you, I know you not. Watch therefore, for ye know not the day nor the hour" (Matt. 25:1-13).

2. Parable of the Talents.

"For *it is* as *when* a man, going into another country, called his own servants, and delivered unto them his goods. And unto one he gave five talents, to another two, to another one; to each according to his several ability; and he went on his journey. Straightway he that received the five talents went and traded with them, and made other five talents. In like manner he also that *received* the two gained other two. But he that received the one went away and digged in the earth, and hid his lord's money. Now after a long time the lord of those servants cometh, and maketh a reckoning with them. And he that received the five talents came and brought other five talents, saying, Lord, thou deliveredst unto me five talents: lo, I have gained other five talents. His lord said unto him, Well done, good and faithful servant: thou hast been faithful over a few things, I will set thee over many things; enter thou into the joy of thy lord. And he also that *received* the two talents came and said, Lord, thou deliveredst unto me two talents: lo, I have gained other two talents. His lord said unto him, Well done, good and faithful servant: thou hast been faithful over a few things, I will set thee over many things; enter thou into the joy of thy lord. And he also that had received the one talent came and said, Lord, I knew thee that thou art a hard man, reaping where thou didst not sow, and gathering where thou didst not scatter; and I was afraid, and went away and hid thy talent in the earth: lo, thou hast thine own. But his lord answered and said unto him, Thou wicked and slothful servant, thou knewest that I reap where I sowed not, and gather where I did not scatter; thou oughtest therefore to have put my money to the bankers, and at my coming I should have received back mine own with interest. Take ye away therefore the talent from him, and give it unto him that hath ten talents. For unto every one that hath shall be given, and he shall have abundance: but from him that hath not, even that which he hath shall be taken away. And cast ye out the unprofitable servant into the outer darkness: there shall be the weeping and the gnashing of teeth" (Matt. 25: 14-30).

The thoughts brought out in the parable of the ten virgins and the parable of the talents, are well expressed in this motto which Mr. H. J. Heinz has frescoed on his private study:

"Work every day as though you would live forever:
Live every day as though you would die to-morrow."

3. Parable of the Tares.

"Another parable set he before them, saying, The kingdom of heaven is likened unto a man that sowed good seed in his field: but while men slept, his enemy came and sowed tares also among the wheat, and went away. But when the blade sprang up and brought forth fruit, then appeared the tares also. And the servants of the householder came and said unto him, Sir, didst thou not sow good seed in thy field? whence then hath it tares? And he said unto them, An enemy hath done this. And the servants say unto him, Wilt thou then that we go and gather them up? But he saith, Nay; lest haply while ye gather up the tares, ye root up the wheat with them. Let both grow together until the harvest: and in the time of the harvest I will say to the reapers, Gather up first the tares, and bind them in bundles to burn them; but gather the wheat into my barn" (Matt. 13:24-30).

4. Parable of the Dragnet.

"Again, the kingdom of heaven is like unto a net, that was cast into the sea, and gathered of every kind: which, when it was filled, they drew up on the beach; and they sat down, and gathered the good into vessels, but the bad they cast away. So shall it be in the end of the world: the angels shall come forth, and shall sever the wicked from among the righteous, and shall cast them into the furnace of fire: there shall be the weeping and the gnashing of teeth" (Matt. 13:47-50).

II. JUDGMENT IS NECESSARY AND UNIVERSAL

1. Necessary.—Judgment is a necessary part of life as we know it. There is order in the universe, a place for all. Every one will finally go to his place; that is, judgment. The separation of men according to character is constantly going on. In any community one can see the law working that draws persons of like character together. The law works imperfectly here, but beyond there will be no hindrances to its operation.

2. Universal.—If judgment is necessary, it is equally necessary for all. Jesus declares that it is universal.

"And before him shall be gathered all the nations: and he shall separate them one from another, as the shepherd separateth the sheep from the goats" (Matt. 25:32).

Paul declares the same:

"And reckonest thou this, O man, who judgest them that practice such things, and doest the same, that thou shalt escape the judgment of God?" (Rom. 2:3).

Men may escape the judgment of our courts, but they can not escape the judgment of God.

III. JUDGMENT IS NOW IN PROGRESS

Sometimes we think of judgment as an entirely future event. Perhaps that is the reason why some expect to escape by a late repentance.

"All things therefore whatsoever ye would that men should do unto you, even so do ye also unto them: for this is the law and the prophets" (Matt. 7:12).

"For judgment is without mercy to him that hath showed no mercy: mercy glorieth against judgment" (Jas. 2:13).

"And forgive us our debts, as we also have forgiven our debtors" (Matt. 6:12).

IV. GOD IS THE JUDGE THROUGH CHRIST

1. God the Judge.—Paul declares that God is to be the Judge.

"But thou, why dost thou judge thy brother? or thou again, why dost thou set at nought thy brother? for we shall all stand before the judgment-seat of God. For it is written,
As I live, saith the Lord, to me every knee shall bow,
And every tongue shall confess to God.
So then each one of us shall give account of himself to God" (Rom. 14:10-12).

2. Christ the Judge.—Paul also says Christ is to judge.

"For we must all be made manifest before the judgment-seat of Christ; that each one may receive the things *done* in the body, according to what he hath done, whether *it be* good or bad" (2 Cor. 5:10).

3. The Blending of One and Two.—These two statements blend in the following passages:

"For neither doth the Father judge any man, but he hath given all judgment unto the Son" (John 5:22).
"And he gave him authority to execute judgment, because he is a son of man" (John 5:27).

In the last reference the reason for appointing Christ judge is because he was the Son of man as well as the Son of God. He knows the divine will, and he also knows men, their trials and difficulties. Christ himself is to be the test by which character is to be determined and destiny secured.

V. THE LAW OF THE JUDGMENT

We are to be judged according to our works.

"And I saw the dead, the great and the small, standing before the throne; and books were opened: and another book was opened, which is *the book* of life: and the dead were judged out of the things which were written in the books, according to their works" (Rev. 20:12).

The applying of the law of Christ as the test of judgment, is illustrated in the great parable of the judgment. Read Matt. 25:31-46.

VI. PRACTICAL BENEFITS OF SUCH TEACHING

1. All Truth is Wholesome.—If there is to be a judgment, the better we understand it and prepare for it, the better will we fare.

2. It Serves as a Timely Warning.

"Rejoice, O young man, in thy youth, and let thy heart cheer thee in the days of thy youth, and walk in the ways of thy heart, and in the sight of thine eyes; but know thou, that for all these things God will bring thee into judgment" (Eccl. 9:11).

SOME REFERENCE BOOKS

The Gospel Preacher, by Benjamin Franklin, Sermon XX., Vol. I.; *Sermons*, by Charles Reign Scoville, Sermon XI., page 226.

TOPICS FOR HOME STUDY AND CLASS DISCUSSION

1. What is the great lesson taught in the parable of the ten virgins (Matt. 25: 1-12).

2. What great truth is taught by the parable of the talents (Matt. 25: 13-31)?

3. What great truth is taught by the rejection of the goats (Matt. 25: 31, 32)?

4. What do we learn concerning the judgment by the parable of the tares (Matt. 13: 24-30)?

5. What does the parable of the dragnet teach us concerning judgment (Matt. 13: 47-50)?

6. Can a just God punish folks?

7. Discuss the judgment that is now in progress.

8. What is the great law of judgment?

RAPID-FIRE DRILL

Use Questions 170 and 171 in the back of this book.

BLACKBOARD OUTLINE

. PARABLES OF JUDGMENT. 　　1. Ten Vir. 　　2. Tal. 　　3. Tares. 　　4. Drag. III. NOW IN PROGRESS.	II. JUDGMENT. 　　1. Nec. 　　2. Univ. IV. THE JUDGE. 　　1. God thr. Chr. 　　2. Christ.

V. LAW OF JUDGMENT.

VI. PRAC. BEN. OF SUCH TEACHING.

1. All Tr. Who.　　　　　　　2. Ser. as Ti. War.

LESSON XVIII.

The New Testament Church and Christian Union

Never has there been a day since the German Reformation that Christians could sing as truly:

> "We are not divided,
> All one body we,
> One in hope and doctrine,
> One in charity."

I. THE NEED OF CHRISTIAN UNION

The need of Christian union is being felt on every hand, insomuch that it is being put into practice in many ways undreamed of by workers of the last century. Among the many reasons why we need Christian union, we mention four here:

1. The Local Expense.—The expense of a divided church is too great for the amount of work done. We are safe in saying that fully five times as much good could be accomplished with the same amount of money if we had a united church. In a town of six hundred people there are five churches, each of which has a poorly paid minister. They have five houses of worship, any one of which would hold the entire audiences of all the churches combined. They have poor choirs, poor Sunday-schools, poor Young People's Society, and even poor, but earnest, ministers. An onlooker would not think that these churches had anything in common, as they many times speak unfavorably of each other. People without are disgusted, and the people within are at the point of despair. And, indeed, who can censure them? They have wasted money, time, talent and souls, because they have hardened their hearts against the prayer of the Master. Can we not, amidst our confusion, hear him now in the stillness of the garden, as he breathes out that wonderful prayer: "That they may all be one, that the world may believe that thou [Father] didst send me" (John 17: 20, 21). Who is there who does not deplore the existing state of Christendom? The evils just spoken of are not imaginary ones, nor are such cases as the above isolated ones, such as might be exceptions to the general rule or such as might rarely occur. In this town from $3,000 to $6,000 are spent annually *for the Lord*, and goes to pay the ministers who spend two-thirds of their time defending what they themselves admit to be their denominational peculiarities. In this way their time is spent, and their money given *for the Lord* is used in building sectarian walls and thus making a way for the spread of infidelity. The cause of Christ is disgraced by his professed friends. And worst of all, the blame rests almost entirely upon the ministry. Would it not be better for these five churches to retain one of their ministers, then send the other four out as missionaries to preach Christian union? Sell four of the church houses and use the money for spreading the gospel. You say this is not practicable. We ask, "Is it the Lord's will?" Certainly such work as this will be done just as soon as we are willing to say to our great leader, King Jesus, "Thy will, not mine, be done."

2. The Administrative Expense for World-wide Work.—The expense of having one hundred missionary boards when one, or, at most, a few, would do more effective work, is very wrong. There is also the expense of hundreds of small colleges, almost all of which are scantily endowed, while with a united church we could have enough with untold better equipment and advantages. Then with a united church the philanthropic associations could be better and more advantageously carried on.

3. Can Not Save the World.—We need Christian union because a divided church can not *save* the world. Many a person with his heart burning for the truth has been turned to skepticism because of the persistency of sectarianism. Often the missionaries have been asked to state what they wanted the earnest inquirer to believe ere they demanded that he *must* believe in order to be saved. In our endeavor to win the world to the one faith, we do not go about it in a oneness of effort. Christendom presents to the world a divided church because it *is divided*. We are making it manifest to the world that we ourselves are not able always to unite in practical work, or are not even *one* as to what Christianity really is. Our divisions magnify our petty differences until we think them insurmountable. They create a spirit foreign to Christ, and cause embarrassment in every line of Christian work. Our divisions go to the mission fields because there is such a great sectarian element in the Christian life of the times. What happens on the mission field is such as is natural and inevitable under existing conditions. If, again, Christ's purpose was to save humanity, and the present conditions can not do that, then *conditions must change.*

4. We are Misdirecting Our Vital Forces.—We need Christian union because in the wars of sectarianism we are misdirecting our vital forces, and will ever do so as long as the church exists. There is still something in Voltaire's sneer, who said, "You Christians are disputing whether the Holy Ghost proceeds from the Father as well as the Son, whilst multitudes have not even heard if there be a Holy Ghost; whether any infants have been elected from eternity, whilst myriads of infants are growing up in vice and sin; whether the heathen on the other side of the globe will hereafter be saved, whilst the heathen at your door are already lost. You are splitting hairs of theology, with society falling to pieces around you. If this be Christianity, we want none of it. Settle your useless disputes and unite vigorously in improving the world that now is, and then we will listen to your promises of a better world to come."

The writer is certainly stating the facts. What shall we do to remedy them? The church is the light of the world and the salt of the earth. Shall we let this light become dim, or the salt lose its savor? This question is for you to answer.

II. SIGNS OF CHRISTIAN UNION

The associative tendency of our age is very marked. In many quarters this tendency is strong enough to transcend sectarian spirit, and wherever the war on creeds has ceased a true Christian spirit is seen. Two centuries ago it was even dangerous to breathe in secret a word of religious toleration, but to-day we find Christians of every name, and nations uniting their forces to oppose the saloon, political corruption and other mighty evils. In our great conventions thousands upon thousands of Christians are brought together, not under any human name, not impelled by sectarian spirit, but who are acknowledging only King Jesus as their leader, and who are taking as their motto the simple yet wonderful words, "The World for Christ." In every country and in every tongue we hear the harmonious strain:

> "Blest be the tie that binds
> Our hearts in Christian love;
> The fellowship of kindred minds
> Is like to that above."

Signs of co-operation are appearing on every side, so that even those who run may read them. As nation is getting closer to nation, class to class, nationality to nationality, division to division, can we not catch hints of a time when the world will actually be evangelized; when the best thoughts and ideals will be the common property of all, and when truth and righteousness will rule over every nation? It is certainly true that nations, peoples, lives and motives are uniting as never before, but whether or not the church will meet this tendency with her glad message, remains yet to be seen.

To sum up the signs of Christian union, we mention six:

1. The Decline of Denominationalism.—The leaders in all of the religious bodies of Christendom are getting too big to be bound down by party, and realize that Christ and his cause come first and denominationalism second.

2. The Masses are Demanding It.—The great majority of the masses of the congregations of all denominations are willing now to have a united church. This is manifested by their willingness to co-operate in every practical union movement.

3. Bible Study Spreading.—The Bible is studied more extensively now than ever. In one union teacher-training class in Cincinnati there were eighty-one different churches represented. Certainly this is bringing people closer together where they forget differences; for all thoughts are centered upon the Bible and the Christ of the Bible.

4. Creeds are Passing into Disuse.—Recently I asked a very successful teacher of a certain denomination how long it had been since she had seen her creed, and she told me that she had not seen it for seven years, and possibly would not see it for another seven. I asked her what she was teaching her class, and she replied, "The Bible." When all teachers of all denominations teach the Bible, and the Bible only, we shall soon find ourselves together.

5. Geographical Barriers Have Been Removed.—French, German, English and Scottish churches in our country, and in others, are compacted together, using one language and growing into one nationality. This "century of humanity," as Hall Caine calls it, is the century when we are one, with the same interests, aims, hopes, purposes, loves, sympathies, brotherhood and fatherhood.

6. International Interdenominational Movements.
—We are sure that the greatest interdenominational
movement of the past and present centuries is the
International Sunday-school Association. In America
alone, fully fifteen thousand conventions are held
every year. These conventions bring people of all
names and creeds together for the one common purpose, and that is to make the Bible an open book
in the hands of both teachers and scholars. The
Christian people of to-day are uniting not only to
save young America for Christ, but to enlist men
and women in Bible study and in a more effective
Christian service.

In connection with the International Sunday-
school Association we ought to mention all other
union movements, such as Young People's Christian
Endeavor Society, American Bible Society, American
Tract Society, Young Men's Christian Associations,
Young Women's Christian Associations, the Women's
Christian Temperance Union, Anti-Saloon League, etc.

We can not regard these signs as temporary sen-
timents, but rather as a great movement of the
church toward that ideal unity which our Lord had
in view when he established it. We are beginning
to exalt Christ above all party names and creeds,
and to regard him as the only sufficient foundation
for a church universal. So may we not hope that
this spirit of toleration and work of association may
be that which will advance the closer and more
perfect unity which we trust is not far away?

In our next lesson we will consider the union of
all Christians on the New Testament basis.

SOME REFERENCE BOOKS

The Great Controversy, by Ashley S. Johnson; *First Principles*, by M. M. Davis, "The True Church," page 195; *The Gospel Preacher*, by Benjamin Franklin, Sermons XIII. and XV., Vol. I.; *From Darkness to Light*, by various authors, "The Relation of Denominationalism to Christian Union," pages 23 and 24; *Christian Union*, by David R. Shields.

TOPICS FOR HOME STUDY AND CLASS DISCUSSION

1. Plans for Christian union. (See Isaac Errett's tract, *Our Position*, Chapter 4.)

2. The spirit of sectarianism versus the spirit of love. (See tract by F. D. Power on *Christian Union*.)

3. The minister's part in bringing about Christian union. (See tract by F. D. Power on *Christian Union*, last paragraph.)

4. The union movement of to-day. (See tract by Isaac Errett on *A True Basis of Christian Union*.)

5. Human creeds a barrier to Christian union. (See Isaac Errett's tract, *The True Basis of Christian Union*, pages 13-15.)

6. Is baptism a hindrance to Christian union? (See tract on *Christian Baptism*, by B. C. Deweese; and M. B. Hayden's tract, *Facts About Baptism*.)

7. Why do churches require more to be a member of those churches than the Bible requires in order that we may be Christians?

8. The disadvantages of a divided church.

9. The advantages of a united church.

10. The signs of restoration of the New Testament Church.

11. The successes of the movement to restore the New Testament church.

RAPID-FIRE DRILL

Use Questions 172 and 173 in back of this book.

BLACKBOARD OUTLINE

I. THE NEED.	II. THE SIGNS.
1. Local Expense.	1. Dec. of Denom.
2. Ad. Ex. for W-w. Wo.	2. Bible Study Spreading.
3. Can not Save the World.	3. Cr. are Pass. into Disuse.
4. Misdir. our Vit. For.	4. Ge. Bar. have been Rem.
	5. Inter. Denom. Movement.

LESSON XIX.

Restoration of the New Testament Church. A Resume

I. THE NEW TESTAMENT CHURCH REQUIRES OF ME NO OTHER CREED THAN CHRIST

It does not ask me if I believe the Apostles' (?) Creed, or if I will be true to the rules of any denomination, but permits me to say simply, *"I believe in Jesus Christ, the Son of the living God"* (Matt. 16: 16; Acts 8: 37). On this confession of faith the New Testament disciples were baptized in the name of the Father and of the Son and of the Holy Spirit. No one can improve upon this creed. It is all-inclusive and all-sufficient. So simple that the child who has come to the age of accountability can understand

and accept it, and so profound that the deepest student can not fathom its depth.

It is universal. Methodists, Presbyterians, United Brethren, Baptists, Congregationalists, Episcopalians, can all accept it without any mental reservations. Then, lovers of peace and unity, let us say nothing about man-made creeds, with all their irreconcilable differences, and follow God's way. "Choose you this day whom ye will serve."

II. THE NEW TESTAMENT CHURCH HONORS ITS FOUNDER BY WEARING HIS NAME

It is the Scriptural name (Matt. 16: 18), and the name that will unite all Christians. It is dishonoring our Saviour Jesus Christ to take any other name. Before a lady is married to her betrothed it is wrong in the sight of the law for her to wear his name, but after their marriage it is very wrong for her to refuse to wear his name. The church is the bride of Christ. (John 3: 29.) Before a person comes into his church it is wrong for him to wear Christ's name, but after he accepts Christ and is a member of his church it is very wrong in the sight of God not to wear his name. We are not the *only* Christians, but are Christians *only*. If we love our Saviour, we should be glad to wear his name.

III. THE NEW TESTAMENT CHURCH RECOGNIZES NO DIVISIONS

All Christians were originally one. They may again become so. Divisions are wrong (John 17: 21; 1 Cor. 1: 10-13).

IV. THE NEW TESTAMENT CHURCH IS COM-POSED OF BAPTIZED PENITENT BELIEVERS

The steps into Christ are, *believe* (Mark 16: 16), *repent* (Acts 2: 38), *confess* (Matt. 11: 32, 33), *be baptized* (Mark 16: 16; John 13: 5; Acts 22: 16; Matt. 28: 19). No one is old enough to accept Christ till he can first *believe*. This is always the first step.

V. THE BAPTISM OF THE NEW TESTAMENT CHURCH IS THE BURIAL OF THE PENITENT BELIEVER IN WATER IN THE NAME OF THE FATHER, SON AND HOLY SPIRIT

There is only one baptism (Eph. 4: 5). If sprinkling is baptism, I have a right to ask you for Bible authority, and since you can give me no Scripture for it, I must take that which is revealed in God's word. Have you been baptized? If you have gone down into the water (Acts 8: 38), been baptized (Acts 8: 38), come up out of the water (Matt. 3: 16; Acts 8: 38); if your baptism was a figure of a burial (Rom. 6: 4), a planting (covered up—Rom. 6: 5), a resurrection (Rom. 6: 5), then you have Scripturally been baptized. To change the form from immersion to sprinkling or pouring makes it meaningless, and hence robs it of its intended significance. Many people doubt the validity of their baptism if they have been sprinkled or poured, and rightly they ought to if they can not find a reason in God's word. Immersion is not in doubt. When one is immersed he never demands sprinkling or pouring. Thousands who have been sprinkled or poured have demanded immersion. There is a safe ground. If you doubt your baptism, you, and not God, are responsible for your doubt. Are you willing to risk eternity upon a doubt? A few years ago, while J. V. Coombs was immersing a number of persons in California, an old lady came up and said: "Will you immerse me?" Her confession was taken, and as she came out of the water she said so all around could hear: "Now I know I am right, but I have been doubting my baptism for forty years.".

"The conclusion of the whole matter," says L. C. Wilson, in his "History of Sprinkling" (pp. 110-112), "is summed up in these words: If sprinkling water upon a person is Christian baptism, then God has given us the wrong book, for the Bible does not contain one word upon the subject. Let a person who never heard a word said on the subject of baptism, read the New Testament, and he will never get the idea that sprinkling is baptism.

"In the early settlement of Iowa and Nebraska, a missionary was traveling up the Mississippi, on his way to preach to the Indians. On the boat he fell in company with an intelligent Indian, and, after some talk, the preacher gave the Indian a New Testament, requesting him to read it, which the Indian promised to do. They separated. Time passed, and on a future visit to the same place, the preacher fell in company with the same Indian.

"After friendly greetings and mutual rejoicing, the Indian remarked: 'Indian want white man to baptize him.' This was glad news to the preacher, who at once began to make preparations for the solemn rite. A small table was brought and a bowl of water placed thereon. The Indian watched the preparation with great and growing interest. His curiosity being excited beyond control, he asked: 'What is the white man doing?' 'I am getting ready to baptize you,' was the reply.

"The Indian looked puzzled, and remarked: 'How is the white man going to baptize Indian here?' 'I have the water here, and will soon be ready,' said the preacher. The Indian looked at the minister in blank astonishment, and remarked: 'White man can't get Indian in that bowl. How, how, baptize Indian?' 'I will dip my fingers in the water and place a little water on your forehead,' said the preacher. The Indian looked amazed and confounded, and, taking from his pocket a well-worn copy of the New Testament, handed it to the preacher with the significant remark, 'White man give Indian wrong book—white man give Indian wrong book.'

"The Indian had read only the New Testament, and hence had only New Testament ideas on the subject. And as you can not get out of a book something that is not in it, so the Indian could have no ideas about sprinkling water, since it is not in the book. If sprinkling is what Jesus commanded, and what the apostles taught, and what the constitution of the New Testament requires, the preacher did give the Indian the wrong book, for the New Testament we have is entirely blank on this subject."

The Greek word *baptizo* means *to dip* or *to immerse*. No Greek scholar in any century ever translated it *to sprinkle*. The form was changed by man. Choose you whom you will serve, God or man.

VI. THE NEW TESTAMENT CHURCH TAKES THE BIBLE AS THE SUFFICIENT RULE OF FAITH AND PRACTICE
(2 Tim. 3:16, 17)

It is claimed that the denominational confessions of faith, disciplines and creeds are founded upon the Bible. If this is true, we have the Bible, hence we do not need them. If they contain more than the Bible, they contain too much. If they contain less than the Bible, they contain too little. If they contain the very same as the Bible, we don't need them. This, it seems, is sufficient if we are earnestly seeking for a true basis of union.

VII. THE NEW TESTAMENT CHURCH PRESENTS THE RATIONAL PLAN OF SALVATION

All will admit the following proposition: He who believes that Jesus is the Christ, the Son of the living God, repents of his sins, confesses Christ, is baptized in the name of the Father and of the Son and of the Holy Spirit, and lives a pure life, will be saved. This will save every man. It is all that the Bible requires, so let us preach it without any mystery.

VIII. THE NEW TESTAMENT CHURCH PERMITS THE CHRISTIAN TO REMEMBER THE LORD'S DEATH TILL HE COMES BY PARTAKING OF THE LORD'S SUPPER THE FIRST DAY OF EVERY WEEK

Acts 20: 7 tells us that it was the custom of the early disciples to meet together each Lord's Day for this holy purpose. A minister said to me not long since, "I would like to have the Lord's Supper observed oftener, but the canons of my church will not permit me." Oh, my friends, the darkness of sectarianism is getting too thick when we will permit the rules of man to stand between us and our Saviour. The Lord's Supper is the important service of the Lord's Day, for it is there through the love of our Saviour that we meet *as one* to remember him who, although equal with God, "took upon him the form of a servant, and was made in the likeness of men: and being found in fashion as a man, he humbled himself and became obedient unto death, even the death of the cross. Wherefore God also hath highly exalted him, and given him a name which is above every name: that at the name of Jesus every knee should bow, of things in heaven and things in earth and things under the earth; and that every tongue should confess that Jesus Christ is Lord, to the glory of God the Father" (Phil. 2: 7-11).

IX. THE NEW TESTAMENT CHURCH PERMITS ITS MEMBERS TO ENJOY THE FREE-DOM OF THE GOSPEL

Paul says, "Stand fast therefore in the liberty wherewith Christ has made us free," and if he were living to-day I believe he would say, "and be not entangled in the yoke of sectarianism." As a member of the Christian Church, I am permitted to speak where the Bible speaks and be silent where it is silent.

Our motto, in brief, is:

No Name but Christ's,
No Creed but Christ,
No Book but the Bible,
No Plea but the Gospel.

Christ is the all in all. Everything else is subordinated to that divine life. Place him as the center of our plea and life, and the nearer we come to Christ the closer we will be to each other.

X. THE NEW TESTAMENT CHURCH PRESENTS AN INFALLIBLY SAFE WAY

Are we seeking for an infallibly safe way? We have found it. Will you follow it? It may be right or it might be wrong to wear man-made names. All admit that it is right to take Christ's name for the name of the church. It may be right or it may be wrong to make and use human creeds. It is right, as all know, to take the Bible as our rule of faith and practice. Sprinkling may be right (for argument's sake) or it may be wrong. All admit immersion to be the sure and valid baptism. If you doubt your baptism, you can remove that doubt by being immersed, for all accept immersion. Be on the safe side. The divisions of Christendom are wrong (John 17: 21; 1 Cor. 1: 10), and it is the duty of every Christian to live and work for a reunion of all Christians, as it was in the New Testament times. It pleases Satan to see God's forces divided. United we win, divided we fail.

Will you help to restore the New Testament church, in name in ordinance and in life? We may do this by refusing to wear any other name than Christ, to preach any other gospel than Christ, to take no other creed than Christ and to receive no other rule of faith and practice than the Bible. To restore the New Testament church will rule out all of our unholy divisions. It will obliterate all arbitrary and needless distinctions that separate our common humanity. It will give a new impetus to missionary effort. It will enable us to use our forces in blessing rather than in injuring humanity. It will help us to take a firm and definite stand against the saloon and kindred evils. It will awaken a more delicate conscience concerning our relation to Christ and the church. It will hasten the glad day for which Christ prayed and toward which all harmony-loving Christians are looking. It will enable every Christian not to glory in any man, or in any human creed or denomination, or peculiar doctrine, but to say:

> "In the cross of Christ I glory,
>   Towering o'er the wrecks of time;
> All the light of sacred story
>   Gathers round its head sublime."

It will enable each one of us to say with Paul, "I determine to know nothing—save Jesus Christ and him crucified." Then

"How blest and how joyous will be the glad day
    When heart beats to heart in the work of our Lord;
When Christians united shall swell the grand lay,
    Divisions all ended, triumphant His word!"

No human names, no human creeds, no man-made systems, but *"Christ is all and in all."*

"Like a mighty army moves the church of God;
Brothers, we are treading where the saints have trod;
We are not divided, all one body we,
One in hope and doctrine, one in charity.

"Crowns and thrones may perish, kingdoms rise and wane,
But the church of Jesus constant will remain;
Gates of hell can never 'gainst that church prevail;
We have God's own promise, and that can not fail.

"Onward, then, ye people; join our happy throng;
Blend with ours your voices in the triumph song;
Glory, laud and honor unto Christ, the King,
This thro' countless ages men and angels sing."

TOPICS FOR HOME STUDY AND CLASS DISCUSSION

1. The practical value of the creed of the New Testament church.

2. Why we should honor Christ by placing his name upon the church.

3. What the New Testament says concerning divisions in the church.

4. The conditions of membership in the New Testament church.

5. The baptism of the New Testament church.

6. The rule of faith and practice in the New Testament church.

7. The way the Lord's Supper was observed in the New Testament church.

8. The value of the freedom of the New Testament church.

9. The infallibly safe way revealed by the New Testament church.

10. What a restoration of the New Testament church would mean.

11. The people who are pleading for the restoration of the New Testament.

SOME REFERENCE BOOKS

Orthodoxy in the Civil Courts, by J. H. Edwards; *On the Rock*, by David R. Dungan; *From Darkness to light*, by various authors; *Sketches of Our Pioneers*, by F. D. Power; *Sermons*, by Chas. Reign Scoville, "The Impregnable Rock," Chapter I.; *Seeking the Old Paths*, by Robert Moffett, Chapter I.; *The Great Salvation*, by E. V. Zollars, Chapter I. of the Appendix.

BLACKBOARD OUTLINE

I.	No Creed but Christ.	VI.	The Bible the Rule.
II.	No Name but Christ.	VII.	Rati. Pl. of Salva.
III.	No Divisions.	VIII.	L. S. Each Week.
IV.	Cond. of Membership.	IX.	Freedom of Gospel.
V.	N. T. Baptism.	X.	Infallibly Safe Way.

LESSON XX.

Winning Men to the New Testament Church

I. FOUR CLASSES

In your work in winning souls, do not give what you think, but what the Bible says. Truth will convict. You will meet at least four classes of people in your work.

1. Those who are anxious to become Christians, and who simply want to understand how.

2. Those who do not want to become Christians, and who do not want any one to talk with them about the matter.

3. Those whose lives are saturated with sin.

4. Those who are living in a fairly respectable manner, and who are indifferent as to Christian lives.

II. EXCUSES AND HOW TO MEET THEM

Each class must be dealt with in a different way and by different passages of Scripture. The passages here are simply suggestive. Workers are asked to add to them according to the needs of your services.

1. I Am too Great a Sinner; It is too Late Now.

"Come now, and let us reason together, saith Jehovah: though your sins be as scarlet, they shall be as white as snow: though they be red like crimson, they shall be as wool" (Isa. 1:18).

"All that which the Father giveth me shall come unto me: and him that cometh to me I will in no wise cast out" (John 6:37).

"For the Son of man came to seek and to save that which was lost" (Luke 19:10).

2. I Am Good Enough.

"Faithful is the saying, and worthy of all acceptation, that Christ Jesus came into the world to save sinners; of whom I am chief" (1 Tim. 1:15).

"Even the righteousness of God through faith in Christ Jesus unto all them that believe; for there is no distinction; for all have sinned, and fall short of the glory of God" (Rom. 3:22, 23).

"I beseech you therefore, brethren, by the mercies of God, to present your bodies a living sacrifice, holy, acceptable to God, which is your spiritual service" (Rom. 12:1).

"Even so let your light shine before men; that they may see your good works, and glorify your Father who is in heaven" (Matt. 5:16).

3. Not Now: There is Plenty of Time Yet.

"Therefore be ye also ready: for in an hour that ye think not the Son of man cometh" (Matt. 24:44).

"At an acceptable time I hearkened unto thee, And in a day of salvation did I succor thee: behold, now is the acceptable time; behold, now is the day of salvation" (2 Cor. 6:2).

"Come now, ye that say, To-day or to-morrow we will go into this city, and spend a year there, and trade, and get gain: whereas ye know not what shall be on the morrow. What is your life? For ye are a vapor that appeareth for a little time, and then vanisheth away" (Jas. 4:13, 14).

"But seek ye first his kindom and his righteousness; and all these things shall be added unto you" (Matt. 6:33).

"And I will say to my soul, Soul, thou hast much goods laid up for many years; take thine ease, eat, drink, be merry. But God said unto him, Thou foolish one, this night is thy soul required of thee; and the things which thou hast prepared, whose shall they be?" (Luke 12:19, 20).

4. I Do Not Know How to Become a Christian.

"*Believe* on the Lord Jesus Christ, and thou shalt be saved" (Acts 16:31).

"*Repent ye,* and be baptized every one of you in the name of Jesus Christ unto the remission of your sins" (Acts 2:38).

"Every one therefore who shall *confess* me before men, him will I also confess before my Father who is in heaven" (Matt. 10:32).

"He that believeth and is *baptized* shall be saved; but he that disbelieveth shall be condemned" (Mark 16:16).

5. I Do Not Think it Necessary to Confess Christ.

"If thou shalt confess with thy mouth Jesus as Lord,

and shalt believe in thy heart that God raised him from the dead, thou shalt be saved : for with the heart man believeth unto righteousness; and with the mouth confession is made unto salvation" (Rom. 10 : 9, 10).

6. Perhaps I Am Not One of the Elect.

"And the Spirit and the bride say, Come. And he that heareth, let him say, Come. And he that is athirst, let him come : he that will, let him take of the water of life freely" (Rev. 22 : 17).

"He that believeth and is baptized shall be saved; but he that disbelieveth shall be condemned" (Mark 16 : 16).

"This is good and acceptable in the sight of God our Saviour; who would have all men to be saved, and come to the knowledge of the truth" (1 Tim. 2 : 3, 4).

7. The Future Does Not Concern Me.

"And inasmuch as it is appointed unto men once to die, and after this cometh judgment" (Heb. 9 : 27).

8. I Am as Good as Some Folks who are in the Church.

"So then each one of us shall give account of himself to God" (Rom. 14 : 12).

9. It is Too Great a Cross to be Baptized.

"For what doth it profit a man, to gain the whole world, and forfeit his life? For what should a man give in exchange for his life?" (Mark 8 : 36, 37).

"There is no man that hath left house, or wife, or brethren, or parents, or children, for the kingdom of God's sake, who shall not receive manifold more in this time, and in the world to come eternal life" (Luke 18 : 29, 30).

"For whosoever would save his life shall lose it: and whosoever shall lose his life for my sake shall find it" (Matt. 16 : 25).

10. My Business Does Not Make it Possible for Me to Be a Christian.

"And every one that hath left houses, or brethren, or sisters, or father, or mother, or children, or lands, for my name's sake, shall receive a hundredfold, and shall inherit eternal life" (Matt. 19 : 29).

11. I Can Not Give Up All.

"If any man would come after me, let him deny himself, and take up his cross, and follow me. For whosoever would save his life shall lose it: and whosoever shall lose his life for my sake shall find it. For what shall a man be profited, if he shall gain the whole world, and forfeit his life? or what shall a man give in exchange for his life?" (Matt. 16 : 24-26).

12. I Do Not Like that Preacher of Yours.

"Your faith should not stand in the wisdom of men, but in the power of God" (1 Cor. 2 : 5).

13. I Know I Ought to, But—

"To him therefore that knoweth to do good, and doeth it not, to him it is sin" (Jas. 4 : 17).

14. I Am Afraid I Can Not Hold Out.

"Who by the power of God are guarded through faith unto salvation ready to be revealed in the last time" (1 Pet. 1 : 5).

15. I Do Not Know Which Church to Join.

"And I also say unto thee, that thou art Peter, and upon this rock I will build my church: and the gates of Hades shall not prevail against it" (Matt. 16 : 18).
"And the Lord added to them day by day those that were saved" (Acts 2 : 47).

16. I Do Not Know How to be Baptized. Some Folks Say One Thing and Some Another.

"We were buried therefore with him through baptism into death: that like as Christ was raised from the dead through the glory of the Father, so we also might walk in newness of life" (Rom. 6 : 4).
"And he commanded the chariot to stand still: and they both went down into the water, both Philip and the eunuch; and he baptized him" (Acts 8 : 38).
"And Jesus, when he was baptized, went up straightway from the water: and lo, the heavens were opened unto him, and he saw the Spirit of God descending as a dove, and coming upon him" (Matt. 3 : 16).
"Go ye therefore, and make disciples of all the nations, baptizing them into the name of the Father and of the Son and of the Holy Spirit: teaching them to observe all things whatsoever I commanded you: and lo, I am with you always, even unto the end of the world" (Matt. 28 : 19, 20).

17. The World Pays Better Wages than Christ.

"And they that are wise shall shine as the brightness of

the firmament; and they that turn many to righteousness as the stars for ever and ever" (Dan. 12:3).

"For whosoever would save his life shall lose it; and whosoever shall lose his life for my sake shall find it" (Matt. 16:25). See also Matt. 19:29; Rom. 1:16; Luke 18:29, 30.

18. I Do Not Think it Necessary to Observe the Lord's Supper Every Sunday.

"And upon the first day of the week, when we were gathered together to break bread, Paul discoursed with them, intending to depart on the morrow" (Acts 20:7).

"For as often as ye eat this bread, and drink the cup, ye proclaim the Lord's death till he come" (1 Cor. 11:26).

TOPICS FOR HOME STUDY AND CLASS DISCUSSION

Assign each one of the eighteen excuses just given to the different members of your class to report on when this lesson is under discussion. Where the class is large, give two or more people the same excuse.

RAPID-FIRE DRILL

See Questions 174 to 191, inclusive, in the back of this book.

BLACKBOARD OUTLINE

I. FOUR CLASSES.

1. The anxious.
2. The unwilling.
3. The deeply sinful.
4. The indifferent.

II. EXCUSES CONSIDERED.

1. Too great sinner.
2. Good enough.
3. Not now.
4. Don't know how.
5. Confession unnecessary.
6. Not one of the elect.
7. Future uninteresting.
8. Black church-members.
9. Baptism too hard.
10. My business prevents.
11. Too hard.
12. Unpopular preacher.
13. I ought to, but—
14. Can not hold out.
15. Many churches confuses me.
16. Baptism confuses me.
17. Wages too small.
18. Lord's Supper too often.

RAPID-FIRE DRILL

QUESTIONS ON THE NEW TESTAMENT CHURCH.

1. What is the meaning of the word *testament?*

2. Give the fivefold purpose of the Old Testament.

3. Name the divisions of the books of the Old Testament.

4. Give three names for the first five books of the Old Testament.

5. Name the divisions of the books of the New Testament.

6. What are the books of Biography often called?

7. What are the first three Gospels called?

8. Of what does the Book of Acts tell?

9. Why does John say that he wrote his Gospel?

10. What does Paul say in Gal. 3: 24 about the relation of the law and the gospel?

11. What is the Book of Revelation called?

12. Name five methods of studying the Bible.

13. Who wrote the first book of the New Testament?

—14. Give another name for the writer of the first Gospel.

15. What was the name of the apostle chosen to take the place of Judas?

16. What was Matthew's occupation?

17. In what language was Matthew's Gospel most probably first written?

18. In what language was Matthew's Gospel afterwards written, or translated?

19. For what people was Matthew's Gospel written?

20. What main purpose did Matthew have in mind in writing his Gospel?

21. Give two reasons for believing that Matthew's Gospel was written for the Jews.

22. About how many quotations does Matthew make from the Old Testament prophecy as fulfilled in Jesus?

23. What Gospel writer gives the longest account of the Sermon on the Mount?

24. Why does Matthew give such a detailed account of the Sermon on the Mount?

25. What group of parables are recorded by Matthew?

26. Name the parables of the Judgment.

27. Give Peter's confession as recorded by Matthew.

28. Where is Peter's confession found?

29. Give three divisions of Matthew's Gospel.

30. Name two characteristics of Matthew's Gospel.

31. Who wrote the second book of the New Testament?

32. What was Mark's Jewish name?

33. What was Mark's Gentile name?

34. With what two apostles was the writer of the second Gospel intimately associated?

35. What does the Latin word *Marcus* mean?

36. What was Mark's nationality?

37. What was Mark's mother's name?

38. In what city did Mark's mother live?

— 39. Whom does Peter call his "son in the gospel"?

40. Why is Mark's Gospel sometimes called the "Petrine" Gospel?

41. Name two of Paul's traveling companions on his first missionary journey.

42. In what city did John Mark leave Paul and Barnabas and return to Jerusalem?

43. In what province of Asia Minor is Perga?

44. What was the result of Mark's desertion of Paul and Barnabas?

45. How do we know that John Mark again found favor with Paul?

46. What is the shortest Gospel from the standpoint of space occupied?

47. To what people was Mark's Gospel written?

48. Give two reasons for thinking that Mark's Gospel was written to the Gentiles?

49. How much of Mark's Gospel is common matter with the other Gospel writers?

50. Name five characteristics of Mark's Gospel.

51. Who wrote the third book of the New Testament?

52. Of what apostle was Luke a faithful companion?

53. How many times is Luke mentioned by name in the New Testament?

54. According to early tradition, of what place was Luke a native?

55. What was Luke's profession?

56. What was Luke's nationality?

57. Why do we think Luke was a Gentile?

58. How can we tell when Luke was with Paul on his journeys?

59. Why is Luke's Gospel sometimes called the Pauline Gospel?

60. Why is Luke's Gospel sometimes called the Samaritan Gospel?

61. What ministry does Luke emphasize?

62. Why is Luke's Gospel called the Gospel of Prayer?

63. Give five characteristics of Luke's Gospel.

64. Name five miracles peculiar to Luke.

65. Name five parables peculiar to Luke.

66. Where does Luke first join Paul?

67. When does Luke first join Paul?

68. Who is the writer of the fourth Gospel?

69. Name and designate three Johns in the New Testament.

70. Name the Gospel writers who were apostles.

71. Name two apostles who were close companions of John.

72. Name three occasions when Peter, James and John were given special privileges.

73. What two men were called "sons of thunder?"

74. Name the five books in the New Testament written by John the apostle.

75. Name the synoptic Gospels.

76. Why are these Gospels called synoptics?

77. What ministry of Christ does John emphasize?

78. What does Clement of Alexandria call John's Gospel?

79. Make one comparison of the four Gospels.

80. Give one reason why John emphasizes Christ's Judean ministry.

81. What Gospel writer alone records Christ's **first** miracle?

82. What Gospel writer alone gives Christ's first recorded discourse?

83. What Gospel writer represents Christ as the Good Shepherd?

84. What Gospel writer alone records Christ's discourse on the bread of life?

85. Name five characteristics of John's Gospel.

86. What were the two sources of information Luke had in writing the Book of Acts?

87. Give four divisions of the Book of Acts.

88. What is the purpose of the Book of Acts?

89. Around what two great men does much of the history of the Book of Acts hinge?

90. Name five characteristics of the Book of Acts.

91. Name four notable conversions recorded in the Book of Acts.

92. How many people became Christians on the day of Pentecost following the resurrection?

93. Give three names used in the Scriptures for the followers of Christ.

94. What does the word *disciple* mean?

95. Quote a passage of Scripture in which the followers of Christ are called *disciples*.

96. What is the significance of the word *brethren?*

97. Quote the passage of Scripture in which the word *brethren* is used to designate the followers of Christ.

98. From what is the term *Christian* derived?

99. Quote a passage in the Scriptures where the disciples of Christ were called Christians.

100. What does the word *church* mean?

101. Give three names used in the Scriptures for the organization of Christ's followers.

102. Quote a passage of Scripture where the church is called the "church of Christ."

103. Quote a passage of Scripture where the church is called the "church of God."

104. Quote a passage of Scripture where the church is called the "church of the Lord."

105. Quote a verse of Scripture where Christ calls the church "my church."

106. Quote a verse of Scripture where it says that believers are to be baptized in Christ's name.

107. Give two reasons why it is better to wear no other names than those in the Scriptures, both for the church and for the individual members of the church.

108. From what is the word *creed* derived?

109. Why is the question of creed very important?

110. What is the creed of the New Testament church?

111. Give Peter's statement of that creed.

112. Name eight elements of the creed of the New Testament church.

113. What does the word *convert* mean?

114. How may a person know when he is converted?

115. If a person does not believe in the divinity of Christ, what would be the first thing you would tell him to do in order that he might become a Christian?

116. Quote Acts 16: 31.

117. If a person already believes in Christ, what

would be the next thing you would tell him to do in order to become a Christian.

118. Quote Acts 2: 38.

119. If a person already believes in Christ and has repented, what would you tell him to do?

120. Quote Rom. 10: 9.

121. If a person already believes in Christ, has repented of his sins, has confessed him before men, what is the next thing that he must do to become a Christian?

122. Quote Acts 22: 16.

123. Name two ordinances observed in the New Testament church.

124. What does the Greek word *baptizo* mean?

125. What are the prerequisites of baptism?

126. Quote and locate a passage of Scripture showing that faith is a prerequisite of baptism. *Mark 16: 16*

127. Quote and locate a verse of Scripture showing that repentance is a prerequisite of baptism. *Act 2-38*

128. Quote and locate a passage of Scripture showing the necessity of confession. *Matt-10-32*

129. Quote and locate a verse of Scripture showing the purpose of faith, repentance and baptism. *Act 2-3*

130. Quote and locate a passage of Scripture giving authority for infant baptism.

131. Describe Christ's baptism as given by Matthew. *3-15*

132. Describe in the words of Scripture the baptism of the Ethiopian eunuch by the evangelist Philip.

133. In his letter to the Romans, what does Paul say about baptism being a symbol of a burial and resurrection?

134. Quote the words of Christ where he prayed for the unity of all his followers.

135. Name at least four events that took place on the Lord's Day that should cause all Christians to observe it.

136. Why was John baptizing in Ænon, near Salim?

137. Give four names variously used in reference to the Lord's Supper.

138. Why is the Lord's Supper so called?

139. Why is the Lord's Supper called *eucharist?*

140. Why is the Lord's Supper called *sacrament?*

141. Why is the Lord's Supper called *communion?*

142. What two terms are used in the New Testament in reference to the Lord's Supper?

143. Locate a passage of Scripture in which the term *Lord's Supper* is used.

144. Quote and locate a passage of Scripture in which the word *communion* is used.

145. Describe in the words of Paul the observance of the Lord's Supper.

146. About how many times is the term *Holy Spirit* used in the New Testament?

147. Quote a verse in the Scripture where the Holy Spirit is called a Comforter.

148. Name three manifestations of the Holy Spirit.

149. Name the two times when the baptism with the Holy Spirit occurred.

150. When did the church begin?

151. Name two qualifications of an apostle.

152. Quote and locate a passage of Scripture showing that the special twelve whom Christ chose were called apostles.

153. Describe in the words of Paul the qualifications of a deacon.

154. Name two of the most important of the first deacons of the early church.

155. Describe in the words of Paul to Timothy the qualifications of an elder or bishop.

156. What does Paul say in Rom. 12: 1 about our spiritual service?

157. Quote and locate a verse of Scripture showing that giving is reciprocal.

158. Quote and locate a passage of Scripture showing that giving has its heavenly reward.

159. What comment did Christ make upon the widow's mite?

160. Quote and locate a passage of Scripture showing that giving must be cheerful.

161. Quote and locate a passage of Scripture showing that giving must be liberal.

162. Quote and locate a verse of Scripture showing that giving must be systematic, universal and proportionate.

163. What is a missionary?

164. Quote and locate a passage of Scripture showing that the early church had the missionary spirit.

165. Where was Paul when he heard the Macedonian call?

166. Describe this call as given by Luke.

167. Quote and locate Christ's missionary program.

168. What city in Paul's time was the center of a most wonderful missionary work?

169. What great missionary was sent out by this church?

170. Quote and locate a verse of Scripture showing that each one will be judged according to his works.

171. Quote and locate a passage of Scripture showing that each individual will be held responsible to God.

172. Give four reasons for desiring Christian union.

173. Give six signs of Christian union.

174. Quote a Scripture in answer to the person who says, "I am too great a sinner. It is too late for me to accept Christ."

175. Quote a Scripture in answer to the person who says, "I am good enough."

176. Quote a verse in the New Testament in answer to the person who says, "Not now; there is plenty of time yet."

177. Quote four Scriptures in answer to the person who says, "I do not know how to become a Christian."

178. Give a Scripture in answer to the person who says, "I do not think it necessary to confess Christ."

179. If, when you were trying to lead a man to Christ, he would say, "Perhaps I am not one of the elect," what Scripture would you quote?

180. What Scripture would you quote to a person who says, "The future does not concern me"?

181. Quote a Scripture in answer to the person who says, "I am as good as some folks that are in the church."

182. How would you answer a person in Scripture words who says, "It is too great a cross to be baptized"?

183. Give a Scriptural reply to a person who says,

"My business does not make it possible for me to be a Christian."

184. Give a Scriptural answer to a person who says, "I can not give up all."

185. What Scriptural answer would you give to one who says, "I do not like that preacher of yours"?

186. Quote a verse of Scripture in answer to the person who says, "I know I ought to become a Christian, but—"

187. What verse of Scripture would you use to one who says, "I am afraid I can not hold out"?

188. What Scriptural answer would you give to that person who says, "I do not know which church to join"?

189. Give an appropriate Scripture quotation for the one who says, "I do not know how to be baptized. Some folks say one thing and some another."

190. What Scriptural answer would you give to the person who says, "The world pays better wages than Christ"?

191. Quote a verse of Scripture in reply to one who says, "I do not think it necessary to observe the Lord's Supper every Sunday."

192. Give the great commission as recorded by Matthew.

193. Give the "Good Company" Psalm.

194. Name the four great institutions of worship in the Old Testament.

195. Name the three parts of the tabernacle.

196. What furnishings were in the court?

197. What furnishings were in the Holy Place?

198. What was in the Holy of Holies?

199. What is the typical meaning of the court?

200. What is the typical meaning of the Holy Place?

201. What is the typical meaning of the Holy of Holies?

202. What is the typical meaning of the Altar of Burnt-offerings?

203. What is the typical meaning of the Laver?

204. What is the typical meaning of the Golden Candlestick?

205. What is the typical meaning of the Table of Showbread?

206. What is the typical meaning of the Altar of Incense?

RAPID-FIRE DRILL REPLIES

ANSWERS TO QUESTIONS ON THE NEW TESTAMENT CHURCH.

1. Will or covenant.

2. (1) It is a book of history. (2) It shows how God dealt with men in olden times. (3) It shows how God chose a people through whom he might teach the worship of the one God, and through whom in the fullness of time he might send his Son to redeem the world. (4) It is the prophetic photograph of Christ. (5) It is the schoolmaster that brings us to Christ.

"So that the law is become our tutor to bring us unto Christ, that we might be justified by faith" (Gal. 3 : 24).

3. Law, History, Devotion, Major Prophets, Minor Prophets.

4. Law, Pentateuch, Early History.

5. Biography, History, Special Letters, General Letters, Prophecy.

6. Gospels.

7. The "Synoptic Gospels."

8. The Book of Acts tells of the beginning of the church and how we are to become Christians.

9. "But these are written, that ye may believe that Jesus is the Christ, the Son of God; and that believing ye may have life in his name" (John 20: 31).

10. "So that the law is become our tutor to bring us unto Christ, that we might be justified by faith."

11. Apocalypse.

12. (1) Study the Bible as a whole. (2) Study the Bible by books. (3) Study the Bible biographically. (4) Study the Bible according to institutions of worship and service. (5) Study the Bible devotionally.

13. Matthew.

14. Levi.

15. Matthias.

16. Tax-gatherer.

17. Hebrew.

18. Greek.

19. The Jews.

20. To set forth the Messiahship of Jesus.

21. (1) He traces the genealogy of Christ from Abraham and David. (2) He quotes often from the Old Testament.

22. Sixty.

23. Matthew.

24. He desired to show how the law was fulfilled in Christ's gospel. Matthew throughout emphasizes the words of Jesus rather than his works.

25. The parables of the Judgment.

26. The Tares; the Dragnet; Ten Virgins; the Talents; and the Rejection of the Goats.

27. "Thou art the Christ, the Son of the living God."

28. Matt. 16: 16.

29. (1) Genealogy of Christ (1: 1-4: 16); (2) the active ministry of Christ (4: 17-16: 20); (3) closing events of Christ's life (16: 21-28: 20).

30. (1) Written for the Jews. (2) Filled with Old Testament quotations.

31. John Mark.

32. John.

33. Marcus.

34. Paul and Peter.

35. Hammer.

36. Jew.

37. Mary.

38. Jerusalem.

39. John Mark.

40. Mark was intimately associated with Peter, and no doubt gave many things which Peter was in the habit of giving in his discourses.

41. Barnabas and John Mark.

42. Perga.

43. Pamphylia.

44. On his second missionary journey Paul refused to take John Mark with him.

45. During Paul's second imprisonment in Rome he requested Timothy to bring John Mark, saying that he was useful to him for the ministry (2 Tim. 4: 2).

46. Mark's.

47. The Gentiles, and especially to the Greeks.

48. (1) Mark scarcely ever quotes from the Old Testament. (2) Mark adds explanations and translations of words that would be intelligible to the Jews.

49. Fully 93 per cent.

50. (1) Shorter. (2) Does not use prophecy. (3) Descriptions are most vivid. (4) Emphasizes Christ as the Master man of the living present. (5) Written to prove the divinity rather than the Messiahship of Jesus.

51. Luke.

52. Paul.

53. Three.

54. Antioch in Syria.

55. Physician.

56. He was a Gentile, most likely Greek.

57. We gather this from the distinction drawn between him and those "of the circumcision" (Col. 4: 11-14).

58. By the use of the word "we" in his narrative.

59. Because it was written by one who was a very close companion of Paul.

60. Because it is the only one that records the parable of the Good Samaritan.

61. The Perean ministry.

62. Because Luke alone preserves to us the fact that our Lord was praying: (1) When he was transfigured. (2) When the Holy Spirit descended at his baptism. (3) After cleansing the leper. (4) Before calling the twelve. (5) On the cross for the murderers. (6) With his last breath.

63. (1) Gospel of sympathy. (2) Gospel of womanhood. (3) Gospel of thanksgiving. (4) Gospel of prayer. (5) Emphasizes the Perean ministry.

64. (1) Draught of fishes. (2) Widow's son at Nain. (3) Man with Dropsy. (4) Ten lepers. (5) Malchus.

65. (1) Good Samaritan. (2) Rich Fool. (3) Prodigal Son. (4) Dives and Lazarus. (5) Pharisee and Publican.

66. At Troas.

67. On his second missionary journey.

68. John the apostle.

69. (1) John the Baptist. (2) John the apostle. (3) John Mark, the writer of the second Gospel.

70. Matthew and John.

71. Peter and James.

72. (1) At the raising of Jairus' daughter; (2) at the transfiguration; (3) in the agony in Gethsemane.

73. John and James.

74. John, 1 John, 2 John, 3 John and Revelation

75. Matthew, Mark and Luke.

76. Because they to a large extent "take the same view of Christ."

77. His Judean ministry.

78. The spiritual gospel.

79. Matthew represents Jesus as the Wonderful Counsellor; Mark, as the almighty God; Luke, as the everlasting Father; John, the Prince of Peace (Isa. 9: 6).

80. Because it is not emphasized by the other Gospel writers.

81. John (2: 1-12).

82. John (3: 1-21).

83. John (10: 1-21).

84. John (6: 22-7: 1).

85. (1) It differs widely from the other Gospels. (2) Chronological. (3) Emphasizes the Judean ministry. (4) The Gospel of Symbolism. (5) Spiritual Gospel.

86. (1) Personal observation concerning many things. (2) Paul, Philip the evangelist, Peter and James, the Lord's brother, and others.

87. (1) Church in Jerusalem. (2) Church in Tran-

sition. (3) Paul's Preaching Tours. (4) Paul's Imprisonment Work.

88. To tell of the early history of the church, and how men of all classes and conditions were won to Christ.

89. Peter and Paul.

90. (1) Continuation of the Gospel according to Luke. (2) Gospel of the Holy Spirit. (3) Book of Conversions. (4) Christianity spoken of as "The Way." (5) The book hinges around Peter and Paul.

91. (1) Ethiopian eunuch. (2) Paul. (3) Cornelius. (4) Philippian jailer.

92. Three thousand.

93. Disciples, brethren and Christians.

94. Learner. It carries with it the idea of the learner who follows his teacher.

95. "If any man cometh unto me, and hateth not his own father, and mother, and wife, and children, and brethren, and sisters, yea, and his own life also, he cannot be my disciple" (Luke 14: 26).

96. This term has reference to the fraternal relationship among the disciples.

97. "For one is your teacher, and all ye are brethren" (Matt. 23: 8).

98. The term *Christian* is derived from the word *Christ*.

99. "The disciples were called Christians first in Antioch" (Acts 11: 26).

100. The word *church* means "called out" with "from the world" implied.

101. (1) Church of Christ. (2) Church of God. (3) Church of the Lord.

102. "All the churches of Christ salute you" (Rom. 16: 16).

103. "Unto the church of God which is at Corinth" (1 Cor. 1: 2).

104. "The Holy Spirit hath made you bishops to feed the church of the Lord which he purchased with his own blood" (Acts 20: 28).

105. "I also say unto thee, that thou art Peter, and upon this rock will I build my church" (Matt. 16: 18).

106. "Repent ye, and be baptized every•one of you in the name of Jesus Christ unto the remission of your sins" (Acts 2: 38).

107. Party names (1) create; (2) perpetuate divisions in the church.

108. The word *creed* comes from the Latin word *credo*—"I believe.'"

109. The creed dominates the life.

110. Jesus.

111. "Thou art the Christ, the Son of the living God" (Matt. 16: 16).

112. (1) Simple. (2) Profound. (3) Comprehensive. (4) Divine. (5) Pattern. (6) Capable of bringing out our best. (7) Universal. (8) Perfect.

113. To turn again. It is almost equivalent to our expression *right about face.*

114. If he has done what Christ has asked him to do in order to become a Christian, he is converted.

115. Believe. (Acts 16: 31.)

116. "Believe on the Lord Jesus, and thou shalt be saved, thou and all thy house."

117. Repent. (Acts 2: 38.)

118. "Repent ye, and be baptized every one of you

in the name of Jesus Christ unto the remission of your sins; and ye shall receive the gift of the Holy Spirit."

119. Confess. (Rom. 10: 9.)

120. "If thou shalt confess with thy mouth Jesus as Lord, and shalt believe in thy heart that God raised him from the dead, thou shalt be saved."

121. Be baptized. (Acts 22: 16.)

122. "Arise, and be baptized, and wash away thy sins, calling on his name."

123. (1) Baptism. (2) Lord's Supper.

124. To immerse, submerge, to dip.

125. Faith and repentance.

126. "He that believeth and is baptized shall be saved" (Mark 16: 16).

127. "Repent ye, and be baptized" (Acts 2: 38).

128. "Every one therefore who shall confess me before men, him will I also confess before my Father who is in heaven" (Matt. 10: 32).

129. "Repent ye, and be baptized every one of you in the name of Jesus Christ unto the remission of your sins; and ye shall receive the gift of the Holy Spirit" (Acts 2: 38).

130. There is none.

131. "Then cometh Jesus from Galilee to the Jordan unto John, to be baptized of him. But John would have hindered him, saying, I have need to be baptized of thee, and comest thou to me? But Jesus answering said unto him, Suffer it now: for thus it becometh us to fulfil all righteousness. Then he suffereth him. And Jesus, when he was baptized, went up straightway from the water: and lo, the heavens were opened unto him, and he saw the Spirit of God descending as a dove, and coming upon him; and lo, a voice out of the heavens, saying, This is my beloved Son, in whom I am well pleased" (Matt. 3: 13-17).

132. "And as they went on the way, they came unto a certain water; and the eunuch saith, Behold, *here is* water, what doth hinder me to be baptized? And he commanded the chariot to stand still: and they both went down into the water, both Philip and the eunuch; and he baptized him. And when they came up out of the water, the Spirit of the Lord caught away Philip; and the eunuch saw him no more, for he went on his way rejoicing" (Acts 8: 36-39).

133. "We were buried therefore with him through baptism into death: that like as Christ was raised from the dead

through the glory of the Father, so we also might walk in newness of life. For, if we have become united with *him* in the likeness of his death, we shall be also *in the likeness* of his resurrection" (Rom. 6 : 4, 5).

134. "Neither for these only do I pray, but for them also that believe on me through their word; that they may all be one; even as thou, Father, *art* in me, and I in thee, that they also may be in us: that the world may believe that thou didst send me" (John 17 : 20, 21).

135. (1) Christ's resurrection. (2) Descent of the Holy Spirit. (3) Beginning of the church. (4) The disciples met together to observe the Lord's Supper.

136. "And John also was baptizing in Ænon near to Salim, because there was much water there: and they came and were baptized" (John 3 : 23).

137. (1) Lord's Supper. (2) Eucharist. (3) Sacrament. (4) Communion.

138. In honor of him who instituted it.

139. The word *eucharist* means thanksgiving.

140. The word *sacrament* carries with it an idea of an oath or pledge.

141. Because the word *communion* means fellowship, involving the two ideas of contributing and receiving.

142. Lord's Supper and communion.

143. 1 Cor. 11 : 20.

144. "The cup of blessing which we bless, is it not a communion of the blood of Christ? The bread which we break, is it not a communion of the body of Christ?" (1 Cor. 10 : 16).

145. "For I received of the Lord that which also I delivered unto you, that the Lord Jesus in the night in which he was betrayed took bread; and when he had given thanks, he brake it, and said, This is my body, which is for you: this do in remembrance of me. In like manner also the cup, after supper, saying, This cup is the new covenant in my blood: this do, as often as ye drink *it*, in remembrance of me. For as often as ye eat this bread, and drink the cup, ye proclaim the Lord's death till he come. Wherefore whosoever shall eat the bread or drink the cup of the Lord in an unworthy manner, shall be guilty of the body and the blood of the Lord. But let a man prove himself, and so let him eat of the bread, and drink of the cup. For he that eateth and drinketh, eateth and drinketh judgment unto himself, if he discern not the body" (1 Cor. 11 : 23-29).

146. Not less than sixty-six.

147. "But the Comforter, even the Holy Spirit, whom the Father will send in my name, he shall teach you all things, and bring to your remembrance all that I have said unto you" (John 14 : 26).

148. (1) Baptism with the Holy Spirit. (2) Extraordinary gift of the Holy Spirit the apostles were able to

bestow. (3) The ordinary gift or indwelling of the Holy Spirit conditioned upon obedience.

149. (1) On the day of Pentecost following the resurrection (Acts 2:4). (2) At the household of Cornelius (Acts 10:44-46).

150. On the day of Pentecost following the resurrection.

151. (1) Witness of the risen Saviour. (2) Given miraculous power.

152. "And when it was day he called the disciples; and he chose from them twelve, whom he also named apostles" (Luke 6:13).

153. "For they that have served well as deacons gain to themselves a good standing, and great boldness in the faith which is in Christ Jesus" (1 Tim. 3:13).

154. Philip and Stephen.

155. "Faithful is the saying, If a man seeketh the office of a bishop, he desireth a good work. The bishop therefore must be without reproach, the husband of one wife, temperate, sober-minded, orderly, given to hospitality, apt to teach; no brawler, no striker; but gentle, not contentious, no lover of money; one that ruleth well his own house, having *his* children in subjection with all gravity; (but if a man knoweth not how to rule his own house, how shall he take care of the church of God?) not a novice, lest being puffed up he fall into the condemnation of the devil. Moreover he must have good testimony from them that are without; lest he fall into reproach and the snare of the devil" (1 Tim. 3:1-7).

156. "I beseech you therefore, brethren, by the mercies of God, to present your bodies a living sacrifice, holy, acceptable to God, which is your spiritual service."

157. "Give, and it shall be given unto you; good measure, pressed down, shaken together, running over, shall they give into your bosom. For with what measure ye mete it shall be measured to you again" (Luke 6:38).

158. "If thou wouldest be perfect, go, sell that which thou hast, and give to the poor, and thou shalt have treasure in heaven" (Matt. 19:21).

159. "This poor widow cast in more than all they that are casting into the treasury: for they all did cast in of their superfluity; but she of her want did cast in all that she had, even all her living" (Mark 12:43, 44).

160. "Let each man do according as he hath purposed in his heart: not grudgingly, or of necessity: for God loveth a cheerful giver" (2 Cor. 9:7).

161. "He that giveth let him do it with liberality" (Rom. 12:8).

162. "Upon the first day of the week let each one of you lay by him in store, as he may prosper" (1 Cor. 16:2).

163. One sent with a message to another person.

164. "And they went forth, and preached everywhere, the Lord working with them, and confirming the word by signs that followed" (Mark 16:20).

165. In Troas on his second missionary journey.

166. "And a vision appeared to Paul in the night: There was a man of Macedonia standing, beseeching him, and saying, Come over into Macedonia, and help us" (Acts 16:9).

167. "But ye shall receive power, when the Holy Spirit is come upon you: and ye shall be my witnesses both in Jerusalem, and in all Judea and Samaria, and unto the uttermost parts of the earth" (Acts 1:8).

168. Antioch in Syria.

169. Paul.

170. "And I saw the dead, the great and the small, standing before the throne; and books were opened: and another book was opened, which is the book of life: and the dead were judged out of the things which were written in the books, according to their works" (Rev. 20:12).

171. "So then each one of us shall give account of himself to God" (Rom. 14:12).

172. (1) Local expense too great. (2) Administrative expense for world-wide work too great. (3) A divided church can not save the world. (4) We are misdirecting our vital forces.

173. (1) Decline of denominationalism. (2) Masses are demanding it. (3) Bible study spreading. (4) Creeds are passing into disuse. (5) Geographical barriers have been removed. (6) International interdenominational movements.

174. "For the Son of man came to seek and to save that which was lost" (Luke 19:10).

175. "Even the righteousness of God through faith in Christ Jesus unto all them that believe: for there is no distinction; for all have sinned, and fall short of the glory of God" (Rom. 3:22, 23).

176. "Therefore be ye also ready: for in an hour that ye think not the Son of man cometh" (Matt. 24:44).

177. "*Believe* on the Lord Jesus Christ, and thou shalt be saved" (Acts 16:31).

"*Repent* ye, and be baptized every one of you in the name of Jesus Christ unto the remission of your sins" (Acts 2:38).

"Every one therefore who shall *confess* me before men, him will I also confess before my Father who is in heaven" (Matt. 10:32).

"He that believeth and is *baptized*, shall be saved: but he that disbelieveth shall be condemned" (Mark 16:16).

178. "If thou shalt confess with thy mouth Jesus *as* Lord, and shalt believe in thy heart that God raised him from the dead, thou shalt be saved: for with the heart man believeth unto righteousness; and with the mouth confession is made unto salvation" (Rom. 10:9, 10).

179. "This is good and acceptable in the sight of God our Saviour: who would have all men to be saved, and come to the knowledge of the truth" (1 Tim. 2:3, 4).

180. "And inasmuch as it is appointed unto men once to die, and after this cometh judgment" (Heb. 9:27).

181. "So then each one of us shall give account of himself to God" (Rom. 14 : 12).

182. "If any man would come after me, let him deny himself, and take up his cross, and follow me. For whosoever would save his life shall lose it: and whosoever shall lose his life for my sake shall find it. For what shall a man be profited, if he shall gain the whole world, and forfeit his life? or what shall a man give in exchange for his life?" (Matt. 16 : 24-26).

183. "And every one that hath left houses, or brethren, or sisters, or father, or mother, or children, or lands, for my name's sake, shall receive a hundredfold, and shall inherit eternal life" (Matt. 19 : 29).

184. "There is no man that hath left house, or wife, or brethren, or parents, or children, for the kingdom of God's sake, who shall not receive manifold more in this time, and in the world to come eternal life" (Luke 18 : 29, 30).

185. "Your faith should not stand in the wisdom of men, but in the power of God" (1 Cor. 2 : 5).

186. "To him therefore that knoweth to do good, and doeth it not, to him it is sin" (Jas. 4 : 17).

187. "Who by the power of God are guarded through faith unto salvation ready to be revealed in the last time" (1 Pet. 1 : 5).

188. "And the Lord added to them day by day those that were saved" (Acts 2 : 47).

189. "We were buried therefore with him through baptism into death: that like as Christ was raised from the dead through the glory of the Father, so we also might walk in newness of life" (Rom. 6 : 4).

190. "And every one that hath left houses, or brethren, or sisters, or father, or mother, or children, or lands, for my name's sake, shall receive a hundredfold, and shall inherit eternal life" (Matt. 19 : 29).

191. "And upon the first day of the week, when we were gathered together to break bread, Paul discoursed with them, intending to depart on the morrow" (Acts 20 : 7).

192. "Go ye therefore, and make disciples of all the nations, baptizing them into the name of the Father and of the Son and of the Holy Spirit: teaching them to observe all things whatsoever I commanded you: and lo, I am with you always, even unto the end of the world" (Matt. 28 : 19, 20).

193. "Blessed is the man that walketh not in the counsel
    of the wicked,
Nor standeth in the way of sinners,
Nor sitteth in the seat of scoffers:
But his delight is in the law of Jehovah;
And on his law doth he meditate day and night.
And he shall be like a tree planted by the streams of water,
That bringeth forth its fruit in its season,
Whose leaf also doth not wither;
And whatsoever he doeth shall prosper.

The wicked are not so,
But are like the chaff which the wind driveth away.
Therefore the wicked shall not stand in the judgment,
Nor sinners in the congregation of the righteous.
For Jehovah knoweth the way of the righteous;
But the way of the wicked shall perish" (Ps. 1).

    194. Altar, Tabernacle, Temple, Synagogue.
    195. Court, Holy Place, Holy of Holies.
    196. Altar of Burnt-offerings, Laver.
    197. Golden Candlestick, Table of Showbread, Altar of Incense.
    198. Ark of the Covenant.
    199. World.
    200. Church.
    201. Heaven.
    202. Christ's sacrifice.
    203. Christian baptism.
    204. Bible.
    205. Lord's Supper.
    206. Prayer.